NOTES FROM
THE DOCKSIDE

Best Wishes
and more Fishes

NOTES FROM
THE DOCKSIDE

Mike Yurk

Mike Yurk

authorHOUSE®

AuthorHouse™
1663 Liberty Drive
Bloomington, IN 47403
www.authorhouse.com
Phone: 1-800-839-8640

First published by AuthorHouse   07/09/2011

ISBN: 978-1-4634-2868-6 (sc)
ISBN: 978-1-4634-2869-3 (ebk)

Printed in the United States of America

Dedicated To

Ted and Paula Rouse

Tim and Susan Wegener

Pat Ebersberger

And in Memory of

Deacon Norman and Florence Wegener

Tony Ebersberger

CONTENTS

INTRODUCTION

From the very beginning The Notes From The Dockside has been an interesting writing project. When I first began writing these columns I decided that none of the columns would go over four typewritten pages. It could be less but no more. If they went over that then I would edit or rewrite them until they would fit into four pages.

The column recorded my thoughts, observations, and fish stories, for the most part irrespective of the season. Therefore there would be columns about fishing in summer that would appear in winter and, as well, some stories set in winter were published in summer. When it is hot outside, people feel a little better if they read something about the winter and during the winter it makes the cold weather a bit more bearable to occasionally read a story set during the summer.

Since I did not have to conform to any seasonal schedule these columns, for the most part, were published in the order I wrote them. There were times that the stories matched the season but that was more coincidence than design. There are three or four Notes From The Dockside that were not published originally as a column for one reason or another and there is one story that was used in another format that has been added to this collection. With those few exceptions, all of these stories represent the last four years of the Notes From The Dockside and are printed in this volume in sequence as they came off my computer.

I would like to thank Outdoors Weekly for initially taking the chance to let me start this column and to the Hudson Star-Observer for continuing the stories. Thanks also to the readers of both publications for their ongoing interest in the Notes From the Dockside.

Over the years I have had a number of typists who type and retype my manuscripts, helping me to make sense of what I have written. Because of Penny Hoge, Nichole Snyder and Michelle Wyss these manuscripts become books. Thank you ladies.

I would like to thank my parents, Walter and Alice Yurk for their support and encouragement to a young writer, working on his first stories on his father's black standup typewriter. Father was my first editor and Mother typed those early stories so I could send them out to magazines. I would not be where I am today without them.

And especially my thanks and love goes out to my wife, The Bass Queen. Not only does she join me on many of my fishing adventures but she is also my editor. Her suggestions and comments make my writing better and these columns and this book would not be possible without her support, enthusiasm, patience and love.

THE FIRST CAST

The first cast is filled with hope and promise. It is the beginning of a new day. It is the start of another fishing trip. In some cases it might be the opening of a fishing season.

One year on the opening day of the fishing season in Bavaria, I was fishing a pond at Bamburg. My son, Todd, and I were fishing a small, muddy point that jutted out into the pond. It had not been my first choice of spots but one of the few that were open when we got there after driving over an hour from home.

Todd was using the old standby, a night crawler and I was fishing a spinner. On my first cast the spinner jolted to a stop and I felt a fish surge off for the center of the pond. It put up a short but spectacular fight that had the fish flipping out of the water by the time I finally pulled the fish up on the bank. It was a foot long rainbow trout.

A few minutes later Todd had a fish. It was a wonderful beginning to the season and Todd and I ended the day with a half dozen trout that ranged from twelve to fourteen inches. And it all started with the first cast.

The first cast can at times be the indicator of good things to come. Several months after our opening day in Bamburg, we had moved to Minnesota and in early October Todd and I went on our first fishing trip in our new home state.

It was a glorious fall day. We had blue skies overhead with a light wind that ruffled the surface of the lake. It was Indian summer warm. I had heard of this lake from one of the guys that worked with me. Todd and I were going to fish it for the first time.

We motored across the lake to a rocky point that protruded into the lake from a marshy bay. We started on the marshy side of the point and on my first two casts I caught two bass. As we rounded the tip of the point I flipped my crankbait out across the point. I had the bait halfway back to the boat when it just stopped. I pulled back to set the hook and nothing moved. I would have thought that I was snagged but I finally felt movement as a fish just slowly moved off as if it was completely unconcerned with my bait in its mouth. The fish turned out to be a muskie; the first I ever caught.

We rounded the point and on the other side Todd caught a twenty seven inch northern. At that time it was the biggest fish Todd had ever caught. He was a very happy young fisherman.

Another time some dozen years later, Todd and I were fishing for bass at a lake in Wisconsin on a hot summer day. As we pulled up to the first point where I always start on this lake, I told Todd that I needed to check out a new bait on a reel that I had just fixed. My first cast was just going to be an experiment. On the first cast I caught a bass. In fact, on the first seven casts I caught six bass and missed a fish. It was the beginning of the day and we caught and released over sixty fish. After that day the bait I started the day with became one of my favorites and I knew that reel was in fine shape.

But there are times that the first cast can give us false hope. You catch a fish on the first cast and you say to yourself it is going to be a great day. But that doesn't always turn out to be the case. Two of my fishing buddies, Arnold and Doug and I were fishing for smallmouth bass one late summer day. Arnold had never used a tube jig before. I briefly explained how a tube jig worked and Arnold cast his bait out.

I was still rigging one of my rods when Arnold yelled that he had a fish. It was a foot long smallmouth. I mentioned that it didn't take long for Arnold to get the hang of that tube jig and with him catching a fish on the first cast it meant that we were going to hammer fish. We fished for several more hours and Arnold never caught another fish and Doug and I caught only another half a dozen fish and felt lucky to get those.

But more often then that there are no fish or even a strike on the first cast. The first cast leaves us in limbo; questions still unanswered. It is still a good day. It might be another couple of minutes or maybe an hour before the first fish. We might catch lots of fish yet and perhaps only a few. But a new day of fishing has dawned with that first cast and that is always a good thing.

There will always be anticipation with the first cast. That is the way it should be. There should be wonder and excitement to fishing and that adventure always begins with the first cast.

THE RULING

It was an ugly summer sky. It was early evening and my fishing buddy, Doug, and I were fishing a lake not far from home. Above us a black cloud swirled overhead pulling a bright gold cloud into it. Behind it the sky was lime green.

Doug and I were fishing for about an hour. He had one nice bass and I had missed a strike.

We looked around. The land was quiet, eerie quiet. And there wasn't any wind at first and then we could feel a cool blast of air blow across the lake.

"This isn't looking good," Doug finally said.

I had to agree. But I hated to leave. I had not caught a fish yet and I did not want to be skunked. The sky looked as bad as I had ever seen it and I had to admit that the situation was getting dangerous.

It was time to leave; fish or no fish. I reluctantly turned the boat towards the landing. I hated to leave before catching a fish but it seemed foolhardy to stay any longer.

By the time we got the boat back on the trailer and had secured the last strap on the boat the wind had begun to whip around, churning the dust on the road. Within a mile up the road, rain pelted down, drumming on the top of the van. Dark skies made it black as if it was nightfall already. When we hit the first little town on the way home, their street lights were on and waves of rain washed across the road.

"I think we got out at the right time," I told Doug. He agreed.

But it still bothered me that I was skunked. We had only been out for a little over an hour and had fished only a portion of this small lake.

Then it dawned on me. If in baseball they can call a game prior to the fifth inning because of weather it is considered a non game to be played later, then why could we not do the same thing in fishing? As we were driving home, with my van being rocked by the wind and rain, I brought it up to Doug.

We talked it over and made a ruling. If you have fished less than half of the time and water that you had planned on and the weather forces you off the water and you have not caught a fish yet then you can not be skunked. The time is not counted as a fishing trip therefore you can not be skunked if you did not catch a fish. It seemed perfectly reasonable to me.

LANTERNS AND STOVES

It seems that I have spent an inordinate amount of time in my life with lanterns and stoves and I never seem to get them to work right. Something always seems to go wrong with them.

When I commanded my last company in Germany my First Sergeant had this beat up, old lantern that we always took to the field with us. It seemed to work great. My tent was the command tent and my First Sergeant, the Operations Sergeant, my Lieutenant and I slept in it. As was our custom, the first person to get up in the morning would light the lantern and our stove and put a pot of water on for coffee.

One morning, on our last field exercise together, the First Sergeant got up to light the lantern. The lantern was hanging from a rope on the center pole of the tent. He lit the lantern and it flared up as it normally would. But usually in a few seconds the flame would die down and then you could adjust the lantern to get the most light from it.

I was about half awake and watched as the First Sergeant was trying to adjust the flame but this time it did not seem to work. Fire started shooting from the top of the lantern and would not die down. The First Sergeant began to curse as he attempted to put out the flame but the blaze continued to dance out of the top of the lantern. He tried to blow it out but that would not work and then he tried to untie the knot but the flame was so hot that it would not let him do that either.

This was not looking good. This whole tent could go up. I rolled over and reached under the cot for my helmet. At night before I went to sleep, I would throw my wallet, knife, glasses, flashlight and anything else that was in my pockets in my helmet that I set under the cot.

I reached for my knife, opened it up and handed it to the First Sergeant. He grabbed the knife, cut the rope and burst out of the tent, throwing the blazing lantern as far as he could. There he stood outside the tent in his underwear cursing and swearing. Then he looked around and saw the entire company formed up for breakfast at the mess tent and they were all watching him. With all the excitement going on the Lieutenant never woke up.

Stoves can be just as bad. Another time when I was in the field I lit the stove and set the water pot on the stove and stepped outside the tent. I was watching the company setting up. The Operations Sergeant was huddled around a hood of a truck with a handful of other sergeants looking at a map. He looked up and yelled to me that I had a fire in my tent. I turned around to see the top of the field table on fire. Oh shit. I raced in and quickly put it out.

The stove had a small leak in the fuel hose. I did everything to fix it but every now and then it would leak fuel and ignite and of course set the top of the field table on fire. Now I should have gotten another stove. That would have been the prudent thing to do but for some reason I kept hanging onto that old stove.

On my last deployment to Turkey, I got up one of the first mornings that we were there and lit the stove to get the coffee going. I noticed fuel leaking from the side of the stove and it began to spread across the top of the field table and then it flared up into flames.

With that, the Platoon Sergeant, still in his sleeping bag looked up and said "use water, sir." I tried to blow out the flame which normally would work and then I would wipe up the fuel and all would be good.

This time it didn't work but I kept trying. The Platoon Sergeant said again, "use water, sir." His voice was a little louder now.

I tried to blow it out and the flame spread across more of the table. "Use water, sir" he said again and this time he was louder yet.

But I felt it was just a minute or so before the flame would go out and all would be fine. I tried again and still no luck. By this time the entire table top was on fire. This time the Platoon Sergeant screamed, "You got to use water." With that he jumped out of his sleeping bag and grabbed a plastic bottle of water and doused the top of the desk. The flame was now out. A couple of minutes later I tried to light the stove again and it worked fine after that.

We had water all over the plastic ground cloth and it was always squishy after that which made walking around the tent in stocking feet a bit unpleasant. Once again, the Lieutenant never woke up. He seemed to be always missing the excitement.

But my Platoon Sergeant was traumatized. Every morning after that, when I got up to light the stove, he would get out of his sleeping bag and sit on his cot with a bottle of water in hand. We never had any more trouble with the stove after that but my Platoon Sergeant wasn't taking any chances.

GOING TO THE BOAT DOCTOR

It is still winter outside. There are snow drifts on my front lawn and the temperature is below freezing. It seems like a long way from spring yet. But I am beginning to think about spring and fishing.

It is time to visit The Boat Doctor.

I will be leaving for a ten day trip to Mexico in a week and when I get back I am hoping that I can get out on the river for walleye fishing. By that time the weather should be better and I do not want to be wasting time having the boat worked on. So I will now pull the boat out and take it to The Boat Doctor for its annual spring check up.

Our boat is stored in the garage. Since the final fishing trip last fall the boat has become a repository for all sorts of things that need to be stored during the winter. There are boxes with stuff for my wife's rummage sale, other boxes that need to be thrown out, the third back seat of the van, some tools and other odds and ends.

My buddy, Scott tells me that I should be ashamed to be abusing my boat that way. I tell him that I do feel guilty but with only a two car garage there is little that I can do. My wife's car is in the other half of the garage and my van is parked outside. I do have priorities. The boat always comes first before any car or truck.

Before I can get the boat out I need to unload all the junk that has been thrown in it over the winter. When I do this, I apologize to the boat for misusing it and beg its forgiveness.

There have been times that ice and snow covered the driveway. There is an incline in my driveway to get to the road and I wonder, when it is still icy and snow covered, if I am going to get up the driveway dragging the boat. But I have always managed to get to the road.

One year I drove to the Boat Doctor in the middle of a blizzard. At stop signs and stop lights I got some very weird looks from people in the cars and trucks that pulled up next to me. I know that they thought I was nuts but what better time is there to take your boat to The Boat Doctor.

When I see the Boat Doctor I tell him that I will pick the boat back up in a couple of weeks. I tell him that the boat must be stored inside one of their buildings while I'm gone. My wife, The Bass Queen, would never forgive me if something would happen to the boat while we were gone.

I talk to the Boat Doctor about new batteries and a tune up to the engine. And don't forget to check out the electrical connections. It seems that I have more problems with electrical gadgets on the boat then anything else. Also I ask him to look after the trailer.

As I leave, I always feel bad when I leave the boat behind. But I will be back soon and then we will go fishing. Besides the Boat Doctor will take good care of it and make it better.

NUMBERS

I got this comment off the internet. It was attributed to that social commentator, critic and comedian George Carlin. If he didn't say that, it sounds like something he would say.

It was on how to stay young. He said, "Throw out nonessential numbers. This includes age, weight and height. Let the doctors worry about them. That is why you pay them."

There is much truth to that. Numbers seem to dominate our lives in today's world. Everyone wants to know your social security number and telephone numbers. And today most homes have multiple telephone numbers with cell phones and pagers and other gadgets.

There are way too many superfluous numbers floating around our heads. We need to get rid of those numbers and concentrate on the important ones. Such as how many days to the opening day of fishing season? What are the limits? How many days can I go fishing this year? How far is it to my favorite lake? How many fish do I need for a fish fry? How many dozen minnows will I need when I go walleye fishing? How many cases of beer will I need when I do my fly-in-trip to Canada? How many spinning rods do I need to have when I go fishing? How deep is the lake? At what depth will I find fish?

These are important numbers. Anything else especially phone numbers, is completely unnecessary. And let your doctor worry about your blood pressure.

THE PACKERS IN PANAMA

The town square of Los Santos, which in the interior of Panama, is a mass of people; most of them are drunk. It is Carnival time which is Panamas version of Mardi Gras.

We had gotten there a couple of days earlier after fishing for peacock bass at Lake Gatun. A buddy of mine, Ted, is married to a girl from Panama and we were staying with her parents in the town of Los Santos.

It occurred to me, as I looked over the swaying, dancing, singing throng of humanity that covered the town square that Ted, my wife, The Bass Queen and I were probably the only people for many miles around that spoke English as our native language.

About every hour or so the dancing reached a new level of frenzy as two trucks, with bands with horns blaring and dancing girls, at opposite ends of the square began to drive slowly around the center of town. Everyone, jumping up and down, arms around each other and passing bottles of assorted alcoholic beverages, fell in behind the trucks. Fire trucks were staged along the route and would hose everyone down with water. It was a hell of party.

Three weeks earlier, The Bass Queen and I and some other friends watched in Wisconsin as our team, the Green Bay Packers beat the New England Patriots in Super Bowl

XXXI. Outside it was cold and drifts of snow covered the lawn.

But now in Panama we did not have to worry about the cold and snow. I was wearing a Packer baseball cap. I had worn that cap when we had been fishing for peacock bass and I was still wearing it for the big party in Los Santos.

I am walking across the town square being jostled by the multitude of people all jammed together, dancing and singing and drinking. I am about halfway across the square, looking for Ted and The Bass Queen, when I hear someone bellow "Hey, how about those Packers?"

I look around and then hear it again. It is coming from a young man sitting on a stone curb alongside a sidewalk. I walk over and tell him that I am from Wisconsin. He laughs and tells me that he is from San Diego. I guess that there are four gringos in Los Santos. His girl friend was from Los Santos and he was there with her, visiting her family.

I think that it truly means that the Green Bay Packers are the world champions.

OVERLOOKED

It was one of those spots that I have passed by for years. It is an acre or so pond of water that is connected to one of my favorite lakes by a small, shallow trench. It is tough to get into and by late summer it seems to be a weed infested, smelly pothole. Sometimes in the early spring, shortly after ice out, I have gone in there and found bluegills in the shallow water.

However, by the opening of the fishing season I pass it by with little thought. It is too shallow and I seldom ever see anyone fishing in there.

One afternoon I was fishing this lake with my buddy Ben. It was early season and the woods and fields were fresh looking with the bright green of new grass and leaves. Birds chattered somewhere in the distance. It was warm and we were enjoying the comfort of fishing in just a shirt. Most of the day had been sunny but a black cloud had now rolled over us with a possibility of a rain shower.

We were passing by that little ditch that ran into the pond when Ben said to me, "Do you think that would be worth going into?"

My first inclination was to say no. It was a little too late for there to be any fish in that shallow, stagnant pool.

As I looked at the ditch that lead into it I was questioning whether I could even get in there with my boat.

But we had been catching most of our bass in shallow water and as I looked at the pond again I said to myself, "What the heck?" It will only take a couple of minutes to fish it anyway.

"Sure," I said. "Let's give it a try."

I turned the boat into the little ditch and just barely squeezed through by lifting the trolling motor as Ben raised the outboard. With the prop of the trolling motor just barely in the water we pulled ourselves into the pond. Finally I was able to drop the trolling motor down and it wasn't churning up mud from the bottom.

On my first cast a fish slammed my bait and as I set the hook it came splashing to the surface. It was a bass.

"I guess that there are fish in here," I said to Ben.

As we worked our way along the bank, skimming through the quiet surface of the pond, we steadily caught fish. At one point I made a cast and within a couple of turns of the reel a foot long bass attacked my bait. I let the fish fight against the spinning rod and the tip of the rod bounced. I started to bring the fish in when my line went limp and the rod popped back toward me. I had lost the fish.

I cranked on the reel to retrieve my bait and within another half a dozen turns of the reel I saw a flash in the water and felt a fish charge off with my bait. A moment latter I hoisted a foot long bass into the boat.

I had made a cast and caught and lost a fish but before I had brought the bait back to the boat another fish hit it. This has happened to me in Canada a few times but with all the fishing I have done back home it has only happened one other time here. And I thought there were no fish in this little pond that I have ignored for years.

Ben and I made two trips around the pond. I felt that after the first pass that we probably had spooked most of the fish. But I was wrong again. On the second pass we were still catching fish.

It made me wonder how many good fishing spots get overlooked because it just doesn't look right or we have some other preconceived notion that makes us dismiss such places in our mind with the excuse that there isn't any fish in there. And how many times have we fished great looking water where there were no fish just because we overlook and ignore these spots?

And perhaps in life, like in fishing, we lose out when we overlook things.

A BUCKET OF BLUEGILLS

The bluegills were hitting and you pounded them. You have congratulated yourself on what a fine mess of fish you have caught and you are already looking forward to those meals of bluegill fillets.

It has been a great day of fishing but now it is late afternoon. You have put the boat back in the garage and you are tired and hot. In front of you, before you can take a shower and relax for the evening, is a bucket of bluegills.

You stare at it. It is not going to go away. The last thing you want to do is clean all those fish. As much fun as it was to catch them by now they seem like a huge inconvenience. Only a dirty chore that needs to be done. And like all chores you are doing your best to procrastinate. The longer that you look at the bucket of bluegills the more difficult the task seems. Why did you keep all those fish you ask yourself? You now begin to dread cleaning those fish.

There is only one thing to do. Get to work and start cleaning. The longer that you wait and put it off, the worse it is going to get. You sharpen the knife and grab the first fish and lay it on the newspaper. Cleaning a bucket of bluegills begins with the first fish.

Half an hour to an hour later the fish are all cleaned. The remains have been wrapped in newspaper and dropped in the trash can. The fillets have been rinsed in cold water and deposited in plastic bags. You are washing your hands and now you say to yourself, "That wasn't so bad". As you look back on it, the anticipation was worse than the actual job itself.

Life is much like a bucket of bluegills. We dread so many tasks and chores. Some jobs are easier to put off than others but eventually they have to be done; like cleaning the bucket of bluegills.

As tedious a job that it might be and instead of making it worse by dreading it and trying to put them off, if we just get the job done it doesn't seem nearly as bad as we anticipated it would be.

And so when we have a task in front of us, look at it like just another bucket of bluegills. It really won't be as bad as we think it will be if we get right to it and get it done.

THE COINCIDENCE

We had left the cold of Wisconsin in late winter for a trip to Ixtapa, Mexico. We had gotten there in the afternoon and wandered around the resort finding where the restaurants, and pools and, most importantly, the bars were located. We finally got into our room and unpacked and then met a couple, that we ran into on the plane, at one of the bars as the sun was sinking behind an island into the great blue expanse of the Pacific.

The next day was our first full day in Ixtapa. My wife, Becky, The Bass Queen, and I got up the next morning and after claiming two poolside lounges, went to breakfast. After we ate, we returned to the pool and as I was settling down with a paperback book the Bass Queen announced that she was going into the pool. I nodded to her as I turned the first page of the book and watched as she walked over to the pool and lowered herself into the water.

It was a beautiful day. Any day in Mexico in the winter is a beautiful day. But today it seemed especially so. Back home it was probably snowing. But here it was sunny and warm and gentle breezes came in from the ocean with the smell of salt water in the air.

She started walking around the pool and the first person she ran into was a lady named Barbara. After exchanging names usually the next question is where are you from? Barbara was from Denver. The Bass Queen told her we were from Wisconsin.

Where in Wisconsin? Barbara asked.

"A small town called Hudson."

"I know it well," Barbara said. "I grow up in New Richmond." New Richmond is only a few miles away from Hudson. As they continued to talk, Barbara said that she and her husband return to Wisconsin every year for the month of July to their cabin.

The Bass Queen asked where their cabin was and Barbara told her that it was just a small lake.

"Hardly anybody knows where this lake is," Barbara said.

"My husband and I fish a lot. We might know it." The Bass Queen said.

"It is Lake X." The name has been changed to protect the innocent.

It was one of those oh-my-gosh moments.

"That is my favorite lake," The Bass Queen told her. What are the chances of two total strangers from different parts of the country, meet in Mexico and that they both love the same lake. And to make it even a stranger circumstance, Barbara was the first person the Bass Queen talked to on her first day in Ixtapa.

Especially Lake X. Lake X is less than a hundred acres and a little off the beaten path. Barbara described her cottage. We know it well.

A couple of years ago the Bass Queen caught a six pound bass off their dock.

We exchanged addresses and Barbara and her husband, Cal, invited us to stop by for a beer next summer. Cal also mentioned that he was having a tough time finding the crappies on Lake X during July. I offered to show him where the crappies were and we told them to keep a couple of cold beers for us. It is after all a small world.

A PERFECT TROUT FISHERMAN'S MARTINI

My father, Walter Yurk, was one of the best trout fishermen I have ever known. I swear that he could catch trout in a septic tank. He took to trout fishing late in life when he was in his forties but it did not take long before trout fishing became one of his passions.

Also, my father made the best martinis I have ever had. Now I have mixed a lot of martinis myself but in comparison to him I was a rank amateur. He truly was the master.

Several years after he passed away I was going through some of my files and I found several letters from him telling me about his trout fishing adventures. They brought tears to my eyes as I read them again and in one of them he gave me his recipe for the Perfect Trout Fisherman's Martini. It is too good to just keep to myself so I now share it with the world.

My father always felt that a martini was suppose to be dry. The dryer the better and he also felt that gin was to be served chilled, over ice. There were only a few things that he felt were worse then drinking warm gin. My father never felt that vodka was suitable for martinis. It had to be gin.

By my father's recipe you should pour a bottle of vermouth into a trout stream. Then run downstream one mile and collect a gallon of stream water that has now properly diluted the vermouth. Pour this water into ice cubes trays and freeze. Once the ice cubes are now frozen solid, place them into, preferably, a frosted glass and pour in gin and then enjoy.

It is so simple.

I believe that if there is a heaven that it must have trout fishing and my father is still the best trout fishermen there as well. But on Earth his Perfect Trout Fisherman's Martini lives on.

THE SKUNK MONKEY

She calls it the skunk monkey. It is the nagging fear and embarrassment of getting skunked. My wife, The Bass Queen, feels that this skunk monkey clings to her until she catches her first fish of the day.

Every time we go fishing she battles the skunk monkey. She has taken a great deal of pride in that it has been a couple of years since she was last skunked and she can't wait to rid herself of that day's skunk monkey.

Some days it's easier and quicker to lose the skunk monkey than other days. This last opening day of the bass season my wife caught her first fish of the day and of the season on her tenth cast. It was not a particularly big fish but it did not matter. It was a fish and she was able to shed the skunk monkey.

Other days it takes longer. She becomes more anxious and irritable the longer that it takes. Some days it takes an hour or more before she can tear that skunk monkey off her back.

I tell here that she must have faith. She tells me that she does not need faith. She needs a fish.

Then when she feels that first jolt of the day on her spinning rod and sets the hook and a fish tears off, she fears losing it. She becomes bitterly disappointed if she should lose the fish. It is not losing the fish necessarily that bothers her but it is the fact that she has longer to go with the skunk monkey on her back.

When she does get the fish finally alongside the boat, she breathes a sigh of relief. Any fish will do; regardless of size. The skunk monkey has been lifted. It does not matter if she catches another fish or not after that. The skunk monkey is gone for the day.

But it returns the next day that she goes fishing again. Her battle with the skunk monkey never goes away completely. There is always another day and another skunk monkey.

A SOFT RAIN FELL

It was late summer or early fall. The trees had not started to turn color yet but there was a slight chill to the air to remind us that fall was not far off. It was quiet and dark gray clouds hung close to the ground. Even the trees, still green, had a muted, bland look to them on this early evening.

Rain was in the air. The fact that we could not even hear birds singing led me to believe that it would rain soon. The lake and the woods around it had an eerie gloominess to it.

I asked Robert if he had rain gear with him and he told me that he did. The boat rolled off the trailer, splashing into the lake. I handed the rope up to him where he was standing on the dock and I drove the van with the trailer back to the parking lot. Our vehicle was the only one in the lot.

We pulled away from the shore and motored down the lake. Our motor broke the hush of the evening and it sounded unnecessarily loud and obtrusive. When I turned the motor off everything seemed muted again.

We flipped crankbaits against the bank and slowly worked our way along the shoreline. In keeping with the tone of the evening we talked quietly so that we would not disturb the subdued mood.

Slowly and softly a rain began to fall. There was no thunder or lightening with it. It was a light rain. It was enough for us to put on our rain jacket and it added to the stillness.

The fish were hitting and we steadily caught bass but that too seemed softened by the melancholy of the evening. None of the fish were particularly large but they fought well and we were catching enough of them despite the soft rain.

The rain wasn't hard enough to actually make us wet. Instead we just felt damp. Bass slammed into our crankbaits and dove for the bottom. They put up a tenacious battle right up to the side of the boat where they frequently charged under the boat as our light spinning rods doubled over.

Because of the heavy cloud cover and the soft rain it began to get dark early. Mist and fog danced above the water, shifting in the gathering darkness.

I looked down the bank that we had just fished and out of the mist a canoe emerged. In it were three gray-haired ladies trolling the shoreline with an electric trolling motor clamped to the square stern of their canoe. They almost seemed as if they were a part of the mist.

They quietly went by us. They never waved or yelled to us, asking if we were having any luck. They starred toward and seemingly around us like they never even saw us. None of them seemed particularly happy and they looked glum.

I have fished this lake often and I had never seen these ladies before then and have never seen them since that damp, quiet evening. I had never seen that canoe before either. Fifteen or twenty minutes passed and then we saw them again, coming back along the shoreline. Again they never seemed to recognize that we were there. They silently passed us going in the opposite direction.

Robert and I decided to quit fishing. As I was putting away the rods and getting the boat ready for the run back to the landing the ladies once again appeared out of the mist and soundlessly passed us going down the lake again.

I turned the motor over and again the noise of it seemed profane and out of place in the soft rain. I pushed the throttle forward and the boat cut through the still water. I was almost to the landing when the thought of these ladies began to bother me. Once before on this lake, I remembered rescuing two young men whose canoe had been dumped over by the wake of a passing boat.

I sure did not want the wake from my boat to capsize those ladies and on an evening such as this. There would be no one to help them. I have to go back and check on those ladies, I told Robert. I turned the boat around and began to slowly plow through the mist when I saw the canoe again. It was coming back down the lake. They looked like an apparition floating through the mist. I knew that they were safe and I turned the boat back to the landing.

I looked in the parking lot and there were no other vehicles there besides mine. I began to wonder if I really did see those ladies in the canoe but Robert saw it as well and had remarked to me, on the way back to the landing, how strange it was to see them on the lake.

A soft rain fell on this quiet lake as night quickly fell and we finished strapping down the boat in the darkness. Once more I looked out on the lake and wondered where those three ladies in the canoe came from or where they went to.

THE LAUNDEROMAT

The lake rolled in dirty, gray waves frothed with white foam. The wind howled across the lake, whipping it into a furious mass of hostile water that rocked my boat. With the trolling motor I was trying to hold the boat in position to flip a tube jig near a dock but the wind and waves were manhandling my sixteen foot aluminum boat like it was a toy.

"I don't think I can hold the boat here," I yelled to Doug. The roar of the wind made talking out of the question. I had to yell to be heard. "It is way too rough out here. I think we should hang it up and move to a smaller lake that is out of the wind."

"I agree," Doug yelled back. "No bass is worth getting killed over."

Doug started the outboard motor and backed us out as I kept my foot on the trolling motor so we would not be blown into one of the docks. After finally pulling up the trolling motor we began to work our way back to the landing on the other side of the lake.

No matter what speed we tried it was scary. Waves slammed into us and as the spray washed over the front of the boat, the wind caught it blasting it over us. We were drenched.

It was an excruciating and hazardous few minutes before we finally pulled up in front of the landing. I was never so happy to see a boat landing before as I was to see this one. I beached the boat and Doug went to get my van. The landing was so shallow and the wind so turbulent that I could not drive the boat on the trailer.

Once Doug had backed the trailer into the water I waded out with the boat and pulled it on the trailer. I felt a sense of relief once we got the boat onto dry land.

Doug and I strapped the boat down and put away the fishing equipment. We were soaked to the skin and it was windy and cold. We still wanted to fish but there was no way we could as wet and cold as we were.

But I had an idea. I rummaged around the van and I found a pair of shorts and a sweatshirt. There was a small town across the road from the landing and we drove over to it. I was looking for a laundromat. A block or two off Main Street I found one.

There was an older gentleman there as we came in and he gave us strange looks as we sloshed in. I gave Doug the shorts and sweatshirt and he disappeared into the rest room to emerge a few moments later to hand me a soggy mass of his clothes. I threw them in the dryer, pumped some quarters into it and turned it on. Twenty minutes later the dryer stopped and I stuck my hand into it. The clothes were still damp. I dropped some more quarters into it and started it again.

The gentlemen continued to stare at Doug and I. I knew that we were strangers in town but he did seem to watch us with some sense of bewilderment.

Doug's clothes were dry and he changed back into them and gave me back the shorts and sweatshirt. I went into the rest room, peeled off my wet clothes and put on the dry clothes. My clothes and more quarters went into the dryer.

The gentlemen continued to watch us. Perhaps he was afraid that we were going to steal one of the Better Homes and Gardens magazines that were lying about.

Eventually my clothes were dry and I changed back into them. We had lost an hour of fishing time but at least we had dry clothes. As we were getting into the van to leave, the gentleman got up and went to the window to watch us drive off. Apparently we made his day and I am sure he is still talking about the two crazy fishermen who stopped in at the laundromat to dry their clothes one cold, wet summer day.

Doug and I did find another lake to fish and we finished the afternoon catching a bunch of fish. Although we had lost fishing time, it was well worth it. We had dry clothes.

THE ENDLESS SUMMER

It is late afternoon and the sun is searing the lake, hanging high in a cloudless blue sky. It is hot as you would expect in mid-summer and there is a slight breeze that ruffles the surface of the water.

It feels cool enough as we blast down to the end of the lake but as I pull back on the throttle and the boat settles into the water, sending a wake towards shore, the heat envelopes us. The light wind seems to be only blowing hot air.

Tony and I have our routine and as he is adjusting his chair on the casting deck at the back of the boat I am dropping the trolling motor into the water at the front of the boat. As I settle into my chair, I grab the spinning rod with a spinnerbait. Tony has already made his first cast.

We watch our spinnerbaits dart over the weeds, flashing in the clear water. The boat slowly glides through the water. At the southern end of the lake there are docks with boat lifts, a gravel shore that butts up against an old asphalt road and a couple of patches of lily pads.

Our spinnerbaits probe the weeds and every now and then we see a flash of silver in the water or sometimes the bait just seems to disappear and we pull back to set the hook. The fish tear off, pumping against the spinning rod.

They sprint from one direction to another and then come busting to the surface. I pull back on the fish so they won't vault out of the water and throw the hook. The fish swirls on top and dives again.

Finally we get the fish to the side of the boat and haul it in. It is a bright green largemouth bass. The fish is about a foot long; not a particularly big fish but it put up a good fight. The bait gets pulled out of the fish and it is slipped back into the water.

Generally we find that if a fish hits close to the shore then it will be a bass. Sometimes the spinnerbait will be half the way or more back to the boat when we feel a fish hit. On those occasions the fish is usually a northern pike. The northern pike run small in this lake. A five pounder would be considered a very good fish but they are always fun to catch anyway.

We laugh and talk and joke with each other as we fish. We feel as free as the warm wind tonight. We are comfortable enjoying the summer evening and catching fish.

We come to a corner in the lake. It is weedy here and there are a few submerged flooded stumps and then a small bay with a flat area covered in weeds. We flip our spinnerbaits out and work them through the weeds and around the stumps. I make a long cast across a mass of flooded weeds and I see a fish come out and swirl at my spinnerbait. I pull back to set the hook and the fish immediately rockets out of the water, shaking its head and throwing the bait before I could stop it.

We cross a sandy point where we have never caught fish and then begin to work our way along the western shoreline. The sun begins to dip below the trees and the shadows lengthen. Now with the sun going down while sitting in the shadows it seems to feel a little cooler. I take my sun glasses off.

This is a long stretch of fairly productive water and the boat slides across the water as it's getting darker and we keep pitching our baits toward the shore. We are occasionally rewarded by feeling a jolt on the end of the line as a fish hits.

Once the sun disappears it doesn't take long before darkness starts to descend on us and finally there is only enough light for us to motor back to the landing without having to put on the navigational lights. I make one more cast; the last for the night. It has been a good evening of fishing. We caught about two dozen fish.

I lay the rod down and for a moment I look around to savor the last of this summer day. A warm breeze blows across the water. It is still hot from the day and I am comfortable in shorts and a t-shirt. A bright ribbon of yellow in the west hangs above the dark bank of trees.

Tomorrow will be another day like today and the day after that will be the same and the day after that. For a brief moment it seems like summer will last forever.

In my rational mind I know that it will not last long. In six weeks the first trees will start to turn bright red followed by brilliant yellow leaves and then the more subdued browns. Within another six weeks after that we could see ice on this lake.

But for this brief moment as I sit in the front of the boat with warm breezes blowing over me and the last of the summer sun disappearing and the heat of the day still clinging to the night, the summer seems endless. The cold of fall will come soon enough but for right now it is summer and for this fleeting instant, summer seems like it won't end.

THE HOLE IN ONE

If there is a fishing equivalent to golf's hole in one it probably is catching two fish on one bait. As in golfing, some golfers will play the game their entire life and never get a hole in one. A lot of fishermen will fish all their life without ever getting two fish to hit the same bait.

There is obviously some luck in getting two fish to hit the same bait as there is in hitting a hole in one for golfers. A lot of golfers come close. You hit the ball off the tee and it sails onto the green. Once it bounces across the green it can go anywhere. Often it goes to the right or left of the cup and many cases not even close enough to drop in. But every now and then, and it doesn't happen often, it will roll across the green and drop into the cup to the ecstatic delight and sheer amazement of the guy who hit the ball as well as the envy of everyone else in his group and probably all those on the golf course that day.

In fishing, day in and day out and across the lakes, rivers, ponds, ditches and all sorts of waters in this country, there are millions of people catching fish and only a handful on any given day will catch two fish on the same bait. Although, I suppose that there is a recorded case where a fisherman has caught two fish on the same hook, in most cases catching two fish on the same bait requires bait that has two hooks such as a crankbait.

In my boat, I have had only two people catch two fish on one bait. About five years ago on a cold spring afternoon my wife, The Bass Queen, caught two small bass on a Shad Rap. This achievement is recorded in a photo that sits on a book case shelf in my office. Her head is buried in a pulled up sweatshirt hood but the smile fills the picture as she holds in front of her the bait with two bass hooked on it.

The second time was my buddy Arnold from Germany. Arnold took to fishing late in life; he was in his late 60s. Now he visits me every summer for two weeks to go fishing. A couple of years ago, when he was in his mid 70s we were fishing a small lake one hot August evening when he caught two smallmouth bass on a Jointed Shad Rap. I took a photo of Arnold's catch as well.

But in anything that requires luck, luck can be indiscriminate. I have never caught two fish on one bait. I have been fishing for fifty of my fifty seven years and I have fished in several states and several countries and with all that experience and all those hours on the water I have yet to catch two fish at the same time.

I had come close once. I was fishing Deer Lake in Wisconsin's Polk County and I was fishing a stick bait when a small bass came out and hit it. As I set the hook, another fish came out and tried to take the bait away from the first fish but he missed the hooks and then turned away. I was both surprised and bummed. I wanted to catch two fish on the same bait just like every golfer wants a hole in one.

After that, The Bass Queen and Arnold caught their two fish on one bait but not I. I was still in search of the fishermen's hole in one.

One recent hot summer afternoon I was fishing with friends Bruce and his wife Kay. I was fishing a thick, fat crankbait that would only go a foot below the surface of the water. It was just right for this lake as it would skim above the weeds and the bass would bust out of the weeds to hit it.

It was at the end of the day and my trolling motor battery was running out of juice so there was only a few more casts left before we would have to leave. I flipped the bait near a dock and as I was retrieving it a bass flashed out of seemingly nowhere and hit the bait. I pulled back to set the hook and my light spinning rod pumped against the run of the fish. Right behind the fish was another fish following it. Both fish were about twelve inches long. I just let the fish run. Would the other one hit too?

The other fish spurted past the first fish and tried to yank the bait out of the fish's mouth and then he hooked himself on the other treble hook. I now yanked back and shouted for Bruce and Kay to see what I had.

"Grab the camera," Kay yelled to Bruce.

The fish fought hard but within a moment I had them alongside the boat and I could not wait to get the photo. As I was pulling the fish in with the line, suddenly, one of them fell off. I was not going to get my photo.

But I got both fish alongside the boat and I considered them caught fish. Although I did not have photo evidence to prove my claim that I caught two fish on the same bait, I do have witnesses. I could even get them to sign affidavits. A court of law would accept that; my fishing buddies should too.

Like any golfer that has gotten a hole in one, he wants to get another. And so do I. I want to catch two more fish on the same bait but next time I want to get a photo too.

IS GOD AN EDITOR?

It was an early spring evening and I heard a muffled rumble of thunder. A light rain tapped against the windows of my office. I was working on an article about trout fishing. I had started the story the evening before and was now finishing it up.

I looked outside and a gray mist had descended outside from what I could see from my window. It reminded me of many days that I have been trout fishing and it seemed like appropriate weather to set the mood for writing.

In the back of my mind I felt a bit of concern about the thunder. That had been the only sign of really bad weather. We sometimes have power failures here during bad weather but the light rain convinced me that I had nothing to worry about.

As I was getting to the end of the story, I dismissed the threat that the thunder had represented and was busy trying to complete the last paragraph of the story.

I was now on the last sentence of the story. In another moment or two I would be finished and I could print it. It would take no more than five minutes and the story would be ready to send out tomorrow morning in the mail.

Halfway through the last sentence of the story the lights flickered. It was no more than a couple of seconds. But it was enough to wipe out the whole story on my word processor.

I screamed. I yelled. I cursed. It was all gone. Two evenings worth of work was shot in only a couple of seconds. The screen on my word processor was blank. I stared at the screen for a moment; not believing what had happened. Couldn't the power hold out for just five minutes more?

I got up from my office chair and went upstairs to the kitchen and mixed myself a stiff drink. The Bass Queen was sitting at the dining room table. She knew what happened. There had been the flicker of lights and then the screams. She knew that I wasn't having a heart attack. She had surmised I had lost the story that I had been working on.

I was too bummed out to start over right away. I waited until the next night and started the story again. For the next two nights I rewrote the story. The second story went smoothly and I finished it easily the second evening. To my surprise the second story was better than the first version. The next day I dropped it in the mail and two months later it was published.

As I was reading the story in the magazine it hit me. Maybe God really is an editor. He was looking down on what I was writing and said, "Mike, this story sucks. You need to rewrite it. You can do better." And with that the lights flickered.

THE TEXAS RIG STILL ROCKS

There seem to be a lot of fads in bass fishing. Some come and go and a few even manage to hang around forever. I remember once that the big fad was boron rods for bass fishing. It lasted for a couple of years and now I can't remember when was the last time I have seen a boron rod. As someone explained to me, it seems that boron rods tended to disintegrate after prolonged expose to sunlight. This is most inconvenient, especially since bass fishing is an outdoor sport where fishermen and their equipment are usually exposed to a lot of sunlight. Perhaps if bass fishermen fished only at night the boron rod might have survived.

Artificial baits have had more than there fair share of trends as well. I remember back in the 1980s that there was a movement to make crankbaits look as much like natural forage as possible. It seemed that every month another lure maker was making his baits look more and more natural. It was getting to be quite competitive. However, after a couple of years fishermen noticed that although the baits looked like the real thing they weren't catching as many bass as they were with less natural looking baits. One article in a prestigious outdoor magazine theorized that the problem was that the baits were looking too natural and blending in the cover as real forage would, making it difficult for the bass to see.

I remember another unusual bait in the 1980s that was supposedly designed by a well known bass pro. His photo in the advertisement helped to sell many of those baits and I will admit that I bought a couple of them. I never caught a fish with them and I never met another fisherman that caught a fish with that bait either. Just recently, I have seen that bait being introduced again with new colors. It just goes to show that baits are perhaps like men and women's fashions. Wait long enough and they will come back again.

But perhaps the fads and trends in bass fishing are the most prevalent in plastics. Over the years there has been a proliferation of different plastic baits and techniques. Some have survived the test of time whereas others have slowly withered away. One that I remember particularly well was something called the do-nothing worm. It was a plastic worm about the size of a cigarette and it had a couple of hooks in it. You attached it to a three foot long leader that was tied to a swivel. Above the swivel was placed an egg sinker. It would be worked by just casting it out and retrieving it with a slow, steady retrieve. When a fish hit it, you would not set the hook but just reel in faster. I have not heard of the do-nothing worm since I left Alabama twenty years ago so I guess that the do-nothing must have just died out.

Today there are even more crazy and wacky plastic baits and techniques than ever before. Recently I was experimenting with one of those baits and new techniques on one of my favorite lakes. With me that day was a buddy of mine, Shawn.

As we got on the water I told Shawn I was going to be experimenting with this new bait. We outdoor writers have to do that from time to time. I had brought along an extra rod set up with this new bait for him if he wanted to try it. He declined, saying that he was going to stick with his Texas rigged purple plastic worm. How 20th century can you get? The Texas rigged purple plastic worm goes back to the very beginning of plastic worm fishing for bass. It has caught a lot of fish. But this is the 21st Century and it is time to move on.

Shawn caught the first fish of the day. He also caught the second fish and the third fish and finally after he caught six fish I got a strike. He asked if I wanted to switch to a Texas rig. I told him that in the interest of seeking the truth in outdoor journalism I needed to continue to work this new bait. It would begin to work soon. I think Shawn had caught ten fish by the time I got my first bass into the boat.

I felt that I was just getting warmed up and any moment I would begin to slam fish. But that never happened. Shawn steadily caught fish all afternoon and I caught just a handful. In the interest of outdoor journalism I had given this new worm rig its best shot. I can't say that the fish weren't hitting. Shawn was certainly catching fish. The Texas rig had out performed my fancy new worm rig.

In the interest of fairness (we outdoor writers believe in that) I tried that new rig again and I eventually caught a bunch of fish with it. But it sure did have an unpromising beginning.

It just goes to show that the Texas rigged purple plastic worm still rocks; although it may be 20th century. Probably a hundred years from now the Texas rig will still be working when a lot of these other fads will be long forgotten. Maybe I should try the do-nothing worm again. I should still have a few left someplace.

DAZZLED WITH DIVERSIFICATION

You won't find Mosier's City on any Wisconsin state map but it is there. When you look on a map of Wisconsin you will find a small village in the east central part of the state called Redgranite. But for some of us it is not really Redgranite. We call it Mosier's City.

Mosier's City is named after Mosier's Sporting Goods and the wonderfully loveable, friendly, colorful and funny man who started and owned the store. His name was Don Mosier and it was seldom that Don, even well past retirement age and in his mid 80s, missed a day at his store.

I'm not sure if it was the store that kept Don alive or if Don kept the store alive. One seems inseparable from the other.

As unique as Don himself, Mosier's Sporting Goods was no normal sport store. The first clue that you get to its signature character is as you approach the front door. On the large glass window you see the words "We don't bore you with repetition . . . We'll dazzle you with diversification!!!!"

Then you go through the door to that zany and diversified world of Mosier's Sporting Goods. The store had a little bit of everything in addition to sporting goods. Don brought in loads of factory surplus, wholesale and bankrupt stock.

With the exception of perhaps fresh groceries and beer there was little else that could not be found at Mosier's Sporting Goods. If you needed paper tablets, or candles or glass wear or plastic bags or pots and pans or spices or soaps or throw rugs or backpacks or plastic lamps with horses you could find it at Mosier's. The inventory could change from visit to visit depending on the whims and availability of the stock that Don could find.

They have clothing there and I am proud to have a Mosier's Sporting Goods baseball cap. There were gloves and shirts and pants and underwear and long johns and overalls.

There was always a large display of tools and knives. Many of the tools in my tool box and in the car and in my boat came from Mosier's. The same thing for knives. I bought bunches of them from Mosier's and you can now find them in the car, the garage, the basement and the boat or any of the many possible places I might ever need a knife.

Oh yes, Mosier's sold sporting goods. Over the years I bought a lot of rods and reels, sinkers and hooks, nets, crankbaits, spoons and spinners from Mosier's. A quick check in my basement tells me that I have at least ten spinning rods that I bought from Mosier's. There are probably more if I look further.

Through all this diversity was Dan Mosier. He wore blue jeans with suspenders, a long sleeve shirt, baseball cap and cigar as if it was a uniform. If he wasn't shuffling down one of the aisles he would be sitting in a chair behind the counter to talk, tease and laugh with all the people that would come through the door. If there was a no smoking policy for the other businesses in Mosier's City it did not apply to Mosier's Sporting Goods or to Don Mosier. He enjoyed his cigar like he enjoyed all the people that came through that door.

His attitude was contagious. All the people that worked at Mosier's were friendly with a ready smile and a laugh. No matter what had gone wrong in your world prior to walking in the door everything seemed to get better after a couple of minutes at Mosier's. Polka music or the Packer games always played in the background.

I started going to Mosier's some thirty years ago when my Father and I would be driving through Mosier's City on our way trout fishing in western Wautoma County. There would always be a need to stop to get a couple of extra spinners or something that we needed. Even if we really didn't need anything specific we would find something there that we would need.

After I left for the Army and would come home on leave I always had to stop at Mosier's when I drove by. After retiring from the Army and moving to Hudson, Wisconsin, whenever I return to my hometown in Oshkosh we would have to drive right past the store. The Bass Queen and I seldom came past without stopping.

The other day I received a letter from my Mother. When I opened it I found that she had sent me an obituary from her local paper. Don Mosier had passed away. He was 86 years old. Mosier's City will never be the same again.

I am among probably hundreds of people that will miss him terribly. Don and his store was unique and extraordinary. There aren't many stores like Mosier's Sporting Goods or many men like Don Mosier.

We may all be a little poorer for his passing but heaven got a lot more interesting.

AFTER LABOR DAY

For many people Labor Day is the end of summer. With the end of the Labor Day weekend, life changes. No longer do we have the carefree, warm, sunny days of summer.

The kids go back to school right after Labor Day so for them summer, as they know it, is definitely over with. Even for adults the playtime of summer is gone after Labor Day. No more warm sunny days at the cabin, hot weather fishing or listlessly eating watermelon in the evenings and spitting the seeds on the grass. Fall is coming and it is time to settle down and get ready for winter.

With the kids in school, the routine of life changes. There is homework to do in the evenings, football practices and music lessons after school, football games on Friday nights and soccer matches on the weekends. Life gets to be very busy now.

Even for adults the lazy days of summer are now gone after Labor Day. There seems to be an intensity to life now that there wasn't between Memorial Day and Labor Day. After Labor Day life becomes serious again. There is driving the kids around after school from one activity to another. It is getting darker quicker and what little free time that there is seems to get absorbed quickly in the day to day requirements of just working and not playing.

For those of us who are fishing we notice that life on lakes changes dramatically after Labor Day. There are a lot fewer people on the water. But the fishing is getting better with each day after Labor Day and with each day there are fewer and fewer fishermen out to enjoy it.

On the first Saturday after Labor Day I went fishing on my favorite lake close to my home in northwest Wisconsin. I was surprised to see, as I pulled into the landing, that there were no other cars and trailers parked at the landing. I had the entire lake all to myself.

Now that, in itself, is not necessarily a bad thing. But it did strike me as sad that this was such a wonderful day and I was the only one out on this lake to enjoy it.

Football season is now in full swing with high school games on Friday nights, college games on Saturdays and the pros on Sundays. That takes some people off the lake.

The hunting seasons are beginning. Bow season for deer is open. The early waterfowl season and grouse season open soon after Labor Day and once October begins the rest of the hunting seasons will start. That will take more people off the lake.

The weather begins to change too after Labor Day. There will still be the warm days that remind you of summer but there is the unmistakable transition to another season. At night now a blanket feels good when you go to sleep. When driving to the lake in the afternoon you have the air conditioning going and when you come home after dark you turn the car heater on. Shorts and sandals and t-shirts are replaced by blue jeans, real shoes and flannel shirts.

The moon even seems to look different after Labor Day. There seems to be a coldness to it and the dark clouds shifting above seem to bring more storms and wind with it.

The first color comes to the land. Sumacs are turning red to be followed soon thereafter by the other colors on other trees. The water has a chill to it now.

On shore, people begin to take out their docks and with every weekend there are more docks and boats out of the water and pulled up on land. It is another sign that the seasons are changing.

But this time after Labor Day is a good time for bass fishing. The cooler weather makes it pleasant to be on the water and the fish are hitting. It is also the time for big fish and it is after Labor Day until freeze up that I will catch some of the biggest fish of the season. It is the best fishing of the year.

I find it ironic that there is such great fishing and fewer people to enjoy it. But I shall not complain. It leaves more fish for me.

THE BEST WALLEYE DINNER EVER

There are times in ones life when you have eaten a meal and the memory of it lasts forever. Perhaps it is an especially fine steak or prime rib or maybe it is a lobster or some other exotic meal. Many times this memory has as much to do with the restaurant that you ate at or maybe the people you were with.

I have lots of these food memories. There is a place in Kansas City called Arthur Bryant's Barbeque. They make the finest barbeque pork and roast beef sandwich and ribs that I have ever had. The food is so good there that my wife, The Bass Queen and I, are considering driving down to Kansas City simply to eat again at Arthur Bryant's.

There is a place in Key West, Florida called The Blue Heaven. The place has a colorful past that included a stint as a boxing ring where Papa Hemingway refereed boxing matches. But now it is a restaurant and they make a lobster benedict to die for. I will be in Key West in December and I can't wait (it is mid summer as I am writing this) to be at The Blue Heaven for breakfast. There is another place in Key West, called the Half Shell Raw Bar, where they have the freshest raw oysters that I have ever tasted.

I spent ten years in Germany and the food there is always fantastic. I remember a night in a guest house near

Mannheim where The Bass Queen and I and two friends had fresh white asparagus with a cream sauce and a cordon blue that still activates my taste buds. And another guest house in Garmisch on a cool April evening with the Alps towering around us where I had the best white asparagus soup I have ever had in my life.

Closer to home there is a restaurant in Oshkosh, Wisconsin, where I grew up, called the Roxy where they make the best prime rib that I have ever had. And then there is Key's Café in Woodbury, Minnesota where they have the best hot roast beef, pork or turkey sandwich and chicken and wild rice soup in the whole world. In Centuria, Wisconsin, there is a place called Al's Diner. They have a great ham and cheese omelet; add their hash browns and never go hungry.

But when I think of fish, there is one special meal that I think of. I have eaten a lot of fish and I have made a lot of fish dinners but there is one meal of walleyes that rates as the best fish dinner I have ever had.

On my second trip to Canada, one night I made walleye fillets over an open wood fire. I had been grilling fish for years. I had experimented with them years ago with perch and white bass when I was young, growing up along Lake Winnebago. Years later, when I lived in Alabama, I made black bass on the grill. It was the only way that my family would eat them. After that when I lived in North Carolina and I was catching trout, I would make them on the grill and my two daughters still talk about those trout on the grill.

The way that I grill fish is not fancy. I melt butter in a small pot on the grill and then mix it half and half with Worcestershire Sauce. I place aluminum foil over the grill and then punch holes in it with a knife to let the smoke out.

When I fillet the fish, I scale the fish so that the skin stays on rather than skinning the fish. The skin helps the fillet stay together while it is being grilled. I put them on the grill, turn often and baste with the butter and Worcestershire Sauce.

On this particular day in Canada, Tim and I had a good day of fishing. It was a warm, sunny day and we caught a lot of fish. We kept six walleyes and filleted them before the bugs came out real bad.

That night after a couple of bourbons and water, once the bugs settled down, we started a wood fire outside the cabin. I placed a grill with aluminum foil over the coals, set the pan with the butter and Worcestershire's Sauce on the grill and then laid out the fillets. I turned them often and not having a basting brush available (who would ever expect to find one of those in a cabin in Canada) I used a spoon to pour the sauce and butter over the fillets.

As I sat outside cooking over the fire I heard the fire snapping and cracking, and the wind through the pine trees and the wash of waves on the rocks of the shore. It was completely dark around us and thousands of bright lights shined above me in the heavens. After two or three more drinks (what better timer is there) I piled the fillets on a large plate and brought them inside. I doused the fire outside while Tim got us cold beer. There is no other drink that goes better with fish then cold beer.

I do not remember what else we had with the fish but it doesn't matter. Those fish were so good that I could not waste time eating anything else. The fish had a slightly smoky flavor enhanced with the taste of butter and Worcestershire Sauce that did not overpower the delicate taste of fresh walleyes.

It was the best walleye I have ever tasted. Perhaps it was just the time and the place or maybe the perfect wood fire that made it that good. In the years that have passed since then I have tried often to recapture that meal of walleyes. I have come close once or twice but have never equaled those fish I made that night in Canada over a wood fire. Maybe that is the way it should be. One should always have that one special meal that will never be topped. The memory of it will last forever.

COUNTING YOUR BLESSINGS

It is that time of year that is no longer summer but then again it isn't fall yet either. The day is cloudy but there is little wind. There is talk about storms not far off and that discouraged The Bass Queen from coming along today. I made a couple of phone calls but either everyone else I could think of already had plans, or I got their answering machines indicating that they weren't home.

So I go by myself. I thought that the day had the potential for great fishing and I did not want to miss it. It is early afternoon as I push the boat off the trailer and park the van. The lake is flat calm reflecting the early red leaves of the sumacs and the start of the other trees beginning to turn color. It is not cold but it isn't hot either and as I am fishing I find myself taking off and putting on a jacket and never quite able to get it right. It seems chilly when I am fishing without the jacket but then it seems to get too warm shortly after I put it on.

In the first ten minutes I feel a fish hit my crankbait and I set the hook. I feel the fish pull against the rod for an instant or two and then nothing. I have lost the fish. I do not normally get upset with losing fish but I must admit that I do not like to lose the first fish of the day. It seems like a bad omen.

I fish a lot of good water in the next half an hour where I normally always find fish. But not today. I am wondering if there might be something to the bad omen of losing the first fish.

But my confidence is restored when I feel a fish slam my bait. I set the hook hard, determined to get this fish to the boat. It puts up stiff resistance by the time I finally get the fish into the boat. Within a few more minutes I catch another bass. This is more like it, I say to myself.

I finish up the rocky bank with deep water close to it and I hit a shallow, sandy stretch of shore line with a lot of docks and boat lifts. I switch to a pig-n-jig. I fish a number of docks where I have caught fish before but again I find nothing. I go a long time without a strike and then in an open spot between two docks where I normally would not expect to find fish, I see my line moving away. I reel up the slack and set the hook. The fish stays deep but eventually I get him next to the boat. The fish is a chunky largemouth starting to fatten up for cold weather.

I cross to the other side of the lake and start again with a crankbait in deep water that runs along a steep rocky bank. I pick up a fish quickly but then go a long time until the next hit. I am not catching a lot of fish but I keep at it. I catch another fish a few minutes later and then again after a lengthy time I set the hook into another fish.

The fish fights hard. There are no small fish but no big fish either. They all seem to run from a foot in length to no more than fourteen inches. I hit shallow water over a sandy flat and switch to a shallow running bait. I get one strike. I get to a stretch of a hard rocky bottom close to shore and go back to the pig-n-jig. I look up to see a bald eagle burst out of the trees and soar overhead. I watch until it vanishes over the tree line. I catch nothing and go back across to the north end of the lake.

I am running out of time so I fish fast in only deeper water. I pick up an occasional fish. Finally I find myself back to where I had started almost three hours earlier. I catch another bass and do a quick mental count. I have eleven fish. I decide to continue for a few more minutes to see if I can get an even dozen fish.

About fifty yards further down the shore I catch the twelfth fish. It has not been a bad day of fishing. I did catch a dozen fish but I had expected more so I am disappointed.

I drive home with the boat trailer rattling behind my van and as I turn the corner in the road and see my house it hits me. What am I being disappointed about.

It was a nice day to be out fishing. It was cool but not cold. The lake was quiet and I was the only one on it. I saw an eagle and I caught a dozen fish in a little over three hours time. I certainly have worked harder and longer for fewer fish in my life. And I got to the lake and back home safely.

I should count my blessings and be happy. It was a great day of fishing.

A FISH STORY

I have always liked a good fish story. Over the years I have heard, told and written lots of fish stories.

I believe that I got this from my Grandfather. He was a good story teller and he told wondrous stories. He came from that generation that was born before television and even radio. For his generation they enjoyed getting family and friends together and just talking. They didn't need noise or pictures from a box to be entertained. Good companionship, maybe a glass or two of beer and stories were all they needed to have a good time.

My Grandfather also liked to fish and fishing gave him lots of great stories. He taught me to fish and throughout my childhood, whether I was sitting in a boat or anytime that I was with Grandpa, I loved to hear his stories.

One of my favorite stories of his, that I have retold many times over the years, came from his young boyhood. He still lived in Russia then before his parents took him to America in the early 1900s. As best that I can determine, he must have been about five years old at the time and, although very young, this incident made such an impression on him that he remembered it well.

He lived with his family in a small town on the Volga River. One afternoon he was down by the river watching the fishing boats, when one of the boats caught a huge fish in its net. As the fishermen in the boat tried to bring the fish in, it took off, dragging the boat with it. The fish dragged the boat up and down the river for sometime. It apparently attracted the interest of a number of people in town and they gathered along the bank to watch the struggle.

Eventually the fish got into a deep hole in the river and dove. The fishermen cut the ropes to the net. Later they told the people in town that if they did not cut the ropes that they were afraid that the fish was going to pull the boat under.

They suspected that the fish was a huge sturgeon. The Volga River is world renown for its sturgeon population and it is entirely possible that there were, in those days, sturgeon big enough to pull a boat under the water. Many years ago I read an account where they found a twenty-five foot sturgeon in the Volga River. Although this account was written in the old Communist Russian days and, with everything coming from that country in those days, the story is a bit suspect. However, there certainly were huge sturgeon in the Volga River in the early days of the 20th Century and one of them could have been big enough to sink a boat.

Years later, one spring evening, Grandpa and I were fishing on the Fox River near Oshkosh, Wisconsin, when Grandpa set the hook on a fish. The fish just took off. Grandpa yelled that it was a big fish and that I should pull up the anchor. When I got the anchor up, Grandpa just held on with the stiff fiberglass casting rod and heavy black nylon line that he used. The fish pulled the boat. It probably pulled the boat a couple of lengths of the boat when the hook pulled loose. I never thought a fish in Wisconsin could ever get to be big enough to do that. Grandpa thought that he had tangled with a big sturgeon.

Some many years after that, I was fishing in Key West, Florida, when I hooked onto a tarpon. The tarpon was at least six feet long and according to my guide, probably went about eighty pounds. I fought the fish for over an hour before I got it alongside the boat.

At one point, I was just holding on as the fish raced off and the fish turned the boat around. The boat that we were in was no little dingy. We were in a twenty-five foot fiberglass boat that had a car engine in it for a motor. There was some weight there but that fish was able to move that boat. That was one powerful fish and at that instant I remembered, again, Grandpa's story from the Volga River.

I have much to thank Grandpa for. He taught me how to fish and to love a good story and how to tell a good fish story.

SUMMER IN OCTOBER

It is summer but the calendar said it is October. I am driving to one of my favorite lakes and I am wearing shorts and a t-shirt and the air conditioning is on in the van. The temperature hit eighty degrees today and it is warm like summer but as I drive I can see that it is unmistakably October. The bright yellow, red and orange leaves on the trees stand out sharply against the shiny green pine trees. I see a farmer harvesting soybeans and the wind gently sways the golden stalks of corn as if they were waves on a large lake.

The Bass Queen was supposed to be fishing with me but she fell yesterday, landing on her knee. Today her knee is swollen and painful. She has been taking aspirins and putting bags of ice on her knee but it hasn't helped much.

"Go fishing," she tells me. "You won't have days like this for long." She is right. Last week we were wearing jackets when we went outside and one night we put a fire in the fireplace. The weather is an anomaly.

I make a number of phone calls to buddies to see if they can go fishing. Two of them are bogged down with work, one is painting his house and the other one was busy as well.

"Go," The Bass Queen tells me. "You do not want to miss this kind of day." So I get the boat ready, put more ice in her ice pack, bring her more aspirins and give her a good bye kiss.

A warm gentle breeze blows across the lake. It feels like summer. It is hard to believe this weather so I put a jacket in the boat. I motor the boat out of the landing and head to the shallow bay on the southern end of the lake. I had found bass there the last couple of times so it seems like a logical place to start.

I am casting a shallow running crankbait and slowly work my way through the bay. I did not have a strike and I find that unusual but it is hard to break the summer mood. I see a swirl in front of the boat and I look to see a large snapping turtle sink under the water. As a reminder of summer, a fly nails me on the ankle.

I work around a weedy point and back into the another series of bays at the back of the lake. A rock that protrudes out of the water is covered with small painted turtles. I do not ever remember seeing turtles in October before. They must think it is summer too.

I have been fishing for almost forty-five minutes and I am thinking about moving to another part of the lake when I feel the first fish slam into my bait. I set the hook and the fish bolts for the surface and flips out of the water. I think I have lost the fish but when I tighten the line it is still on. It rockets out of the water again and this time clears the surface by three feet, throwing the bait. Although I lost the fish, I must admit that was thrilling to watch.

A couple of minutes later I get another fish and this one I get to the boat. In the next fifteen minutes I catch about half a dozen bass. It encourages me to stay where I am and continue to fish the shallow water.

It seems that I go a long time before the next fish hits and then I get three or four fish in rapid succession. I fish another long time without a strike and then catch several bass within a few minutes. There is a feast or famine character to today's fishing.

I stop for a minute to take it all in. What a gorgeous summer day. And to think that it really is October. I hear the wind rustling the dry colored leaves on the trees and in the distance I hear the sharp cries of crows and from the weedy shoreline the guttural sounds of ducks calling to each other.

I have finished the shallow water in the bays on the southern heel of the lake and now troll along the west bank where the bank drops sharply into deeper water. I switch to a deeper diving crankbait. I have less than an hour left of fishing time but in that time I pick up another five bass. These fish are a little bigger then the ones I found in the shallow water and they put up a hard, feisty fight.

I am hoping for one more fish but I do not get it and my time runs out. As I am putting the rods back in the rod locker a warm summer breeze washes over me. I never did need that jacket. The Bass Queen was right. I would have hated to miss this day.

On the way home I call her with the cell phone. Her knee still hurts. She asks me how I did fishing and I tell her that I got about twenty bass. That is good she tells me and I agree with her. It is very good for such a summer day.

"WHAT DID YOU SAY?"

"Poor bastard," Matt said.

Penny almost jammed on the breaks as she was driving across town, turned to Matt and asked, "What did you say?"

Matt is the thirteen old son of Penny and Penny is the best friend of my wife, the Bass Queen. Because of that, we are like aunts and uncles to Penny's children and every summer Matt spends a week fishing with me.

"I said 'poor bastard'." Matt replied.

"Where did that come from?" Penny asked.

"We just passed a boat for sale and every time I am with Uncle Mike and we see a boat for sale we always say 'poor bastard' because we feel sorry for that poor bastard who has to sell his boat." Matt explained. His explanation was sufficient to get him out of trouble with his mother.

For years, as Matt travels from lake to lake with me we would see a number of boats for sale. Some guy has to sell his boat. Poor bastard. We can only but hope that he is selling his boat to buy a bigger or better boat. But unfortunately, all too often, a man has to sell his boat for a lot of other reasons and he won't be getting another one anytime soon.

He has our sympathies. A man without a fishing boat is like a fish out of water. It is indeed a sad day when he has to put his boat up for sale and we send our condolences by muttering "poor bastard".

As time has gone on we have realized our need to perhaps be more selective in our sympathy. Someone selling a pontoon boat qualifies for a "poor bastard" because people can fish off of a pontoon boat. Fish and ski packages also qualify as do most of the old style runabout type boats since people do fish from those. However, ski boats do not qualify nor do sail boats and certainly not jet skies.

One of my fishing buddies, Scott, was at the grocery store one afternoon and waiting for his girl friend, Sara, to finish some shopping. While he was waiting, he started looking at the for sale ads on a bulletin board at the exit. He was taking great interest in the ad for a fishing boat.

As he was looking at the ad, Sara came up behind him. She took one look at the ad and said "poor bastard."

"You would have been so proud of her," Scott said. To have such a depth of understanding and compassion was just one more reason why Scott felt he should marry her. So shortly thereafter, Scott did ask her to marry him.

A man who is selling his fishing boat is going through a great personal crisis. A cousin of mine told me once that he had gone through two divorces but he felt worse when he had to sell his boat. So we stand in solidarity with our brothers who have to sell their boats knowing that but for the grace of God we could be there too. Poor bastards.

LIQUID SUNSHINE

When I was in the Army we called it liquid sunshine. But now that I have retired from the military I should call it rain; like everyone else does.

This is the day for liquid sunshine. It has been cold and windy with ugly black clouds swirling over head. It is mid September and the early days of fall are beginning. Some of the trees are starting to turn color and strings of geese cross the skies.

My buddy, Scott calls me. "Do I want to go fishing?" I tell him yes. It might rain, bring your rain gear, he tells me. I am supposed to meet him at the landing. I grab a quick lunch, drop a letter off at the Post Office and drive to the landing. This lake is right in town and it takes me only a moment or two to get there.

When I get to the landing, the only car there is Scott's. He has launched his boat and has already been out fishing while waiting for me. He sees me pull up to the landing and runs his boat across the lake back to the landing, pulling it up on the gravel as I carry my equipment down to him.

A light drizzle begins and the quiet surface of the lake is dimpled by rain drops. I make another trip back to the car and pull on my rain gear.

He tells me that the fishing has been slow but he picked up two small bass just before I got there. By the time we pull away from the landing and head back across the lake to a point, where we usually find bass, the rain has picked up and it is now pouring down, splashing on the surface of the lake.

As he pulls back on the throttle and we come to a gliding stop off a rocky point, Scott points out that "we must be the only two crazy people out here today." Over the years, Scott and I have qualified as crazy and we have fished in some extreme weather together. Although Scott and I do not consider ourselves crazy, there have been a number of people who have told us that we must be crazy so perhaps they might have something there.

We pull up the hoods on our rain jackets as the rain slashes down and we begin to flip our crankbaits against the shore. The wind picks up and rain swirls around us. This point, where we always find fish, does not yield a strike today and we remark that we find that unusual.

We start to work down the rocky bank when Scott yells that he has a fish. I look up through the portal in the hood of my rain jacket and see that Scott's casting rod is bent double. There is a swirl on the surface of the water and I see a flash in the water that looks like it is a good size fish and then his bait comes flying out of the water. He lost the fish. I sympathize with him. No one likes to lose a nice fish.

The wind and rain become worse. I see a steady stream of water running off the bill of my cap. We are encased in hoods so it is difficult to hear the other person when they are talking. I tell Scott that I think he is mumbling. Scott tells me that he is not mumbling and that I am deaf.

I hear Scott cursing. This I hear very clearly. I ask Scott what is the matter. He tells me that he feels a leak in his rain gear. I sympathize with him again. It is never any fun when your rain gear leaks.

A few minutes later Scott yells that he has a fish and he pulls a bass into the boat. By the time that we finish that stretch of bank Scott has two fish. As we are crossing to the other side of the lake Scott mentions to me that he needed his hat to get washed anyway.

On another rocky point I pick up a bass. It does not seem possible but the rain and wind is even getting worse. We fish on and we do pick up a couple more bass. Rain splatters on my glasses, obscuring my vision at times and pounds on my rain gear, drumming on the hood.

Scott waxes philosophical, "Some days you are the bug and some days you are the windshield," he says. I did not ask him which one we were today.

We fish our way back to the boat landing and decide to fish one last point. We each catch a fish on the point. Our total is about a dozen fish. As we motor back to the landing Scott says "this still is better than work."

We are cold and wet, where the rain got through our rain gear, and our fish were small and not as many as we had hoped for but it was fishing and it sure did beat working. Perhaps if we think of it as liquid sunshine instead of rain the whole day seems brighter.

WATER

I recently returned from visiting my old stomping grounds in the mountains of North Carolina. I had lived for three years in the late 1980s and I taught ROTC at a small college. We were staying at a small chalet along a trout steam that I had fished when I lived there. I immediately noticed that the stream was very low and in fact lower then I ever remembered seeing it. The manager of the chalets told me that they, as well as several surrounding states, had been undergoing an extreme drought.

Five days later we found out that the city close to our chalets had instituted several new water conservation measures that included banning any of the motels from renting out rooms with hot tubs or jacuzzis and that all restaurants could only serve food on paper plates with paper or throw away plastic cups and flat wear so they would not waste water by washing dishes.

A couple of days later in Charlotte, we woke one morning to find a note under our door telling us that due to city wide conservation measures the water in the motel would be cut off from eleven that morning until one in the afternoon.

When we returned home, my wife, The Bass Queen, called her niece who lives in Atlanta, Georgia. Her niece told her that if they didn't get any rain soon that they could be out of drinking water by Christmas. This is not a little dry period during the summer when they restrict watering lawns. This is a real drought that could have a major city like Atlanta out of drinking water.

It is hard to believe that this kind of thing can happen in our country. During this last summer we, in the Midwest, experienced a drought. It destroyed great numbers of crops that will have a ripple effect until at least next summer. We were saved from a worse drought by the early fall rains that brought major rivers such as the St. Croix and the Mississippi River to almost flood stage. However, it was too much too late for many of our farmers.

For those of us who hunt and fish, having a enough water and clean water is an issue near and dear to our hearts. For farmers it is a matter of livelihood. In other parts of the world it is a matter of survival.

It has occurred to me that too many Americans take water for granted. We are fortunate to live in a country where we can turn on a water faucet and not only get all the water we want but it is clean, healthy water that won't make you sick to drink it. Some water from various parts of our country may taste better then other places but with little exception it won't make you sick.

I can tell you that this is not the case in many other parts of this world. I know this from first hand experience. I have been deployed while I was in the Army to such places as Turkey and Saudi Arabia and having since retired, traveled in Mexico and Central America. In these places you can not even brush your teeth from tap water without risking getting very sick. The only water that is safe to drink is that which comes from a sealed bottle.

We have seen this happen briefly in our country usually only during disasters. Shortly before I retired from the

Army, I was sent to Iowa during the flooding in 1993 to help with the relief effort. People were standing in long lines with plastic bottles to get fresh water from trucks. This is something that we do not see often in this country.

Water is not only important for drinking but we need it for every part of our existence. We had a couple of people in Des Moines that were staying at a motel. The water plant had been flooded and the entire city had no water. When our guys checked into the motel the clerk gave them buckets and told them that when they needed to flush the toilets to get a bucket of water out of the swimming pool. Showers were out of the question.

We brought in a number of Army water purification units. One unit was solely dedicated to providing fresh water to the zoo. Without it all the animals would have died. That is a rather small and controlled environment. Think of all the farm animals that we have and how much water they need.

Having a well is not completely safe either. I was talking to one man that told me that several people in his area were digging new wells. The existing wells were going dry. There also have been numerous cases where wells, thought to be safe, were contaminated by seepage from old and forgotten landfill sites.

Water is a matter of survival. We need a continuous source of fresh, clean, drinkable water to not only maintain the way of life that we have but to just simply live. Our country has been very lucky in this world that we have what we need but we need to keep an eye on the future to make sure that we keep it. Water for us in the future may become as important as oil is for us now. Like any other resource, if we waste it we won't have it for long.

Do not take water for granted.

WHEN THE BASS GODS SMILED

It had not been a good summer for The Bass Queen. We got a call on Memorial Day weekend. Her mother had collapsed at home on her back porch and had been taken to the hospital. A number of telephone calls later The Bass Queen became increasingly concerned. She packed her suitcase and I drove her back to her childhood home on the other side of the state.

Things did not look good when we got to the hospital. Her mother was very sick and had been diagnosed with a couple of different cancers. At first it did not look like she was going to survive the weekend. But she did. At 85 she was a tough, resilient lady. By the end of the weekend she was doing much better. However, the prognosis did not look good. The Bass Queen decided that she needed to stay for awhile. I returned home alone and went back to work.

We talked everyday on the phone. Some days were better than others. Some days were worse. Her mother would need to go into a nursing home. The Bass Queen was devastated. Her mother had lived alone for several years since the Bass Queen's father had died. It was the house that he had built with his own hands. He had even dug out the basement by hand to save $200. The Bass Queen's parents had lived together in that house for a half a century and had raised four children there.

Now her mother would have to go to a nursing home; away from the things that were hers that she had lived with for her entire life. Away from the kitchen where she had cooked countless Thanksgiving Day dinners, the den where she would watch television in the evening, the bedrooms her children had grown up in, the books that she read, the garden where her husband planted roses.

All that was replaced with a room she would share with another elderly lady. The evening after her mother was moved to the nursing home, The Bass Queen called me. She was hysterical and crying so badly that I could not understand a word that she was saying.

But the nursing home was not bad. The Bass Queen's mother had wonderful, sensitive and caring nurses and her mother was getting a lot of attention. It made the Bass Queen feel better. But the prognosis still was not good. The Bass Queen felt that she needed to be close to her mother so I would send her back by plane or drive her back for what would become weeks at a time. She nursed and cared for her mother. One weekend I came back and we checked her out of the nursing home and took her back to her home for a couple of days. The Bass Queen's brother and I grilled ribs and corn on the grill and we all sat on that back porch and talked about times past.

It was Labor Day weekend. The summer was coming to an end. The Bass Queen returned to our home. She desperately needed a rest and to take a break from the stress. She woke up one morning and looked outside to see bright sun and deep blue skies.

"I want to go fishing," she said. She had not been fishing for a long time and the season was rapidly slipping away.

We went to her favorite lake. She sat in the back of the boat on the casting deck. She was wearing her swimming suit and soaking up as much sun and warm breezes as she could. It was a grand and glorious day and we caught fish. We caught a lot of fish.

We slowly moved the boat along the shore line with the trolling motor and cast crankbaits. The fish hit hard and fought well. They were starting to fatten up for the winter and they were aggressive. All those antiseptic days in the hospital and nursing home and the worry and stress and fears melted away.

The Bass Queen laughed and that smile, that I first fell in love with, returned. I had not heard that laugh or seen that smile for most of the summer. Her light spinning rod bounced in her hand as fish pulled away and the water boiled as fish swirled on the surface.

On the way home, later that afternoon, The Bass Queen said, "It has been a great day. I had fun." The bass gods smiled that day and gave The Bass Queen the gift of a great day of fishing and warm, sunny weather that temporarily took away the worries and troubles that had consumed her summer.

The summer had been difficult and there were more difficulties to come but for one glorious afternoon the only thing that mattered for The Bass Queen was when she was going to catch the next bass. She needed that day. The bass gods smiled on her.

A HOT WIND BLEW

It is summer and it is hot and dry. Even the wind is hot and dry as it blows down the river, between the woody shoreline on one side and the built up bluff of Prescott, Wisconsin on the other. The wind ruffles the surface of the water but there is no relief from this wind. It has that parched, sauna like feel to it as it washes over me while I am pushing the boat off the trailer into the Mississippi River.

As the boat slips off the trailer, I pull on the bow line dragging the boat to the floating dock. Dennis drives the trailer out of the water and parks the van in the parking lot. Dennis and I are old Army buddies and now we fish together. We will fish this stretch of the Mississippi River, trolling crankbaits, along the rocky shoreline south of the boat landing.

We do this several times during the summer. It has been our escape from the normal routine. We meet after work, leaving all of that behind, and fish until dark. It does make for a long day and we seldom get home much before ten at night. But it is interesting that the next day we never feel tired. Such is the rejuvenating powers of spending an evening fishing with a good friend.

I crawl into the boat, starting the motor as Dennis walks back across the parking lot. His feet sound heavy as he walks across the dock and then I feel the boat push off as he steps off the dock onto the deck of the boat.

We motor slowly away from the dock and I pull out two rods with crankbaits that are already attached and hand one to Dennis. We each cast the baits on opposite sides of the boat and start trolling, following the current downriver.

Once we had just started trolling, perhaps no more than twenty five feet and barely away from the dock, when Dennis yelled that he had a fish. It turned out to be a keeper walleye. Whenever we start, we reminisce about that night. It would never seem the same if we didn't.

We troll downstream until we pass a rocky bluff and then turn around in front of a marina and start back upriver over the same water that we just fished.

Even with the heat, it is nice to be on the river. I'll take hot winds on the river while fishing any day over sitting in front of the air conditioning. Dennis and I have been doing this for a number of years. Sometimes Dennis and I fish alone and other times Dennis brings along a colorful assortment of friends. They all work for the Minnesota state government and there is much talk of politics as we fish. There always is much laughter and teasing and remembrances of other fishing trips.

There are times that we have caught a bunch of fish but more often than not we catch only a fish or two and once or twice have been skunked. But the numbers of fish caught or not caught have never been the measure of a good evening of fishing. We have always had good fishing and it has much more to do with the company than with the fish.

Hot winds continue to blow and the sun gradually begins to slip behind the trees. Shadows lengthen; the sky turns gold with streaks of black in it. I look around. It is pretty to be on the river and I notice that we are the only boat on the water.

We catch a fish. It is a sauger and we drop it in the livewell. A few minutes later we catch another. This time it is a walleye. When a fish hits a bait that is being trolled on a long line it seems to slam that bait. The bait stops and the rod is bent double. It could be a snag and I usually wait for a moment. If it is a snag there will be no movement. However, if it is a fish I will feel a thumping as the fish tries to pull away.

Then I pull back the throttle into neutral and everyone pulls in their baits. There is flurry of activity as we drop rods on the bottom of the boat and grab the net and if it is dark enough the flashlight. While this is all going on the boat is drifting downriver with the current.

The navigation lights on the boat are now on and it is dark. One side the shoreline is just a mass of black shadows and tress. On the other side where the town stretches along the bluff, lights shine into the darkness from the bars and the condos and the marina and restaurant that sit along the river. The river has a slick charcoal color to it as the boat plows through it and the water rushes past us on its way south.

We have a couple of fish in the livewell. We caught fish and had a good time. We talked and there was laughter. It was a good night of fishing. It has been a fine way to spend a hot summer night. We will make one more run, trolling along the rocky shoreline, which will lead us back to the boat landing. In the darkness a hot wind blows down the river.

LISTENING TO THE CRICKETS

Gentle breezes ruffle the surface of the water. It is a warm summer night. My neighbor, Tom and I are fishing for bass. The lake we are fishing is only about twenty minutes from our homes. It is a clear water lake with a very pronounced weed bed that circles the shoreline.

I like to fish this lake in the evening. Not only is it close to home but it is also easy to fish and on most evenings we can easily catch a couple of dozen bass with a few small northern for a little extra excitement. The lake does not normally produce many big fish but it does produce a lot of bass in that eleven to thirteen inch category and they are always fun to catch.

Generally I have found that spinnerbaits seem to work well on this lake. Plastic worms will also work well but generally I just use them around docks and boat lifts but I stick with the spinnerbait for most of the lake.

We work the weed beds, moving slowly with the trolling motor as we flip spinnerbaits across the weeds. The water is clear enough that many times we see the fish come flying out of the weeds in a flash of silver and hit our baits. That is always exciting.

On the outside of the weeds the bottom dramatically drops into deeper water. And there are times that bass on the outside of the weeds will come out of the deeper water to slam our lures with a vengeance. It has seemed to me that when they are coming out of deeper water they have such a speed going that it just seems that the strikes are a lot harder.

On this particular evening, however, Tom and I are having a tough time finding the fish. We have found a few fish but not in the numbers that we normally see. Earlier in the evening I had caught a sixteen inch bass and for this lake that is a huge fish. But we threw a lot of spinnerbaits and plastic worms in places that we normally always find fish and came up empty handed.

I am disappointed and starting to get irritated with it. I expected better and I am unhappy with our catch.

It is now starting to get dark. The sun has slipped behind the trees and the shadows are longer, stretching out across the water. There isn't much time left and I feel a sense of intensity as it is getting darker. I start to fish faster, trying to cover more water and thereby get more hits and hopefully more fish. I miss a fish and find myself getting angry that I lost a fish. I do not normally feel that way and it makes me stop for a moment, surprised at my reaction.

As I am sitting in the front of the boat I notice that the crickets are making quite a racket. Interspersed with the sharp clatter of the crickets is the deep rumble of an occasional bull frog. It is a pretty sound in the gathering darkness and I enjoy listening to it.

I am embarrassed as I listen to nature's music. I was so wrapped up in catching fish and becoming upset because I wasn't catching as many fish as I thought I should have that I was losing sight of what a wonderful night that it is.

Life is too short and who knows how many more of these evenings like this we might have in our life. I hope that I will have many more but then again everything can change in an instant. If that is the case I want to enjoy this one more.

I feel chastised and I begin to fish slower and find myself listening more to the crickets and worrying less about how many fish I am catching or not catching. It is getting darker and the sun disappears, reflecting bright gold colors to the underside of the clouds. There is not much time left before we will have to head back to the boat landing.

As I sit back and relax I suddenly find that the fishing begins to pick up. Several fish come flying out of the weeds to hit the spinnerbait and they fight hard, splashing on the surface of the water. I switch to a top water plug and a couple of bass boil up to the surface and suck in the bait. They put up a spectacular fight on the surface before I bring them in the boat.

In these last few minutes I find that the fishing turns around completely. Perhaps it is because it has gotten later in the evening and the fish have just turned on right before dark. Or perhaps it is something more. Maybe it has something to do with me. Once I learned to relax, enjoy the evening, listen to the crickets instead of being concerned with the number of fish I was catching then I truly began to fish.

Fishing is more than just catching fish. It is enjoying the moment. It is listening to the crickets. In a few days I probably will forget how many fish that I caught but I won't forget the sound of the crickets on that hot summer evening.

BOB'S RULE

It is winter. Everything seems frozen in our beloved northland. It is time to go south. So The Bass Queen and I go to Mexico where the beaches are clean, the sun is warm, the ocean is inviting, the rum drinks are icy (rather than the roads) and where you can go fishing on the open sea.

We are in Ixtapa. The Bass Queen has already done some internet exploring about the fishing possibilities. Of course the fish are always biting, according to the websites that she has visited.

It is our first afternoon there and we are still waiting to get into our room. We find a bar. What else would one do? We order a rum drink and find our travel representative to check on finding a fishing boat. While we are waiting for our rep to show up we meet another couple. Their names are Bob and Linda. They were on our plane and after we get talking we find that they live only a couple of hours away from our home in Hudson.

Bob wants to fish. So let's get a boat together. The ocean calls us. Our rep does show up and of course he knows just the right captain and the right boat. We tell him the day we want to go fishing. He calls the captain and yes he is open that day. We give him money and the four of us go find a bar to celebrate our good fortune.

Several days later, it is early morning and still dark outside when we meet in the hotel lobby to get a cab to take us to the small fishing village of Zihuatanejo where our captain and his boat is waiting for us. The Bass Queen was supposed to go along but she got sick the day before so she bows out on our fishing adventure.

Bob, Linda and I hop in a taxi which is always an exhilarating experience. As we are hurtling down the tight streets, we are thankful that there are few people and animals out at this time of the morning. But at the pier there is much excitement and activity. On our pier we see a group of people sitting with a pile of bait fish in front of them to sell to the fishermen as they are getting their boats ready for a day of fishing. A few feet in front of the piles of fish laying on the pier, is a semicircle of cats, sitting and waiting patiently for someone to throw them a fish or two that they can't sell. It is obvious that everyone knows the routine so they just wait quietly.

We find our captain and the boat. The boat is hugging the pier and with the mate's help we get pulled into the boat. The land falls behind us as we motor out of the bay and both the sea and the land are black in the darkness. We see the lights from the hills where Zihuatanejo sits as the town is coming awake. It is still dark but the east is just turning bright orange as the first lines are dropped down. Fifteen minutes later the first rod springs to life and then a second. Bob and I pull in a couple of tuna that measure about two feet long. That is our bait. We are looking for bigger fish.

We spend the rest of the morning dragging those two tuna along behind the boat. The ocean is rolling and so are our stomachs. The breeze feels good and the sun is warm. It has been a fine boat ride. But we want fish. Finally our stomachs stop rolling. I guess that we found our sea legs.

A few minutes later, Bob reaches into the ice chest and pulls out a beer.

"If we want to catch a fish we must have a beer," he says. Apparently he has some experience in these matters. He fishes in Canada and on the Great Lakes and he tells me that if the fish aren't hitting, drinking beer will always bring a change to your fishing luck. "It's Bob's rule," he tells me.

I don't think that Bob finished the beer when suddenly one of the thick, heavy trolling rods begins to jerk in the rod holder at the back of the boat. The mate grabs the rod and pulls back on it several times. He points at Bob to sit down in a chair and he hands the rod to him. Bob pulls back and this pool cue like rod is bent double and the heavy line begins to pull off the real as the fish tears off.

Linda and I get out of the way as the mate begins to clear everything out of the back of the boat. I think that is what they call clearing the decks for battle. And a battle it is. The fish swirls on the tip of the water sending spray high into the air. Bob is straining against the rod as the drag on the reel whines as the fish tears off line. He turns the fish and then the fish tears off again. The fish stops and Bob starts to bring the fish in but again the fish races off.

This goes on for a long time but finally Bob is starting to get the fish closer and now both the captain and the mate are at the back of the boat. The fish is alongside the boat. It is a long, sleek, powerful marlin. The captain estimates the fish to be about a hundred and fifty pounds. It looks a lot bigger to me.

The fish is finally tied to the back of the boat, the rods are pulled in and we start back to shore. Bob has another beer. This one is not for luck but to celebrate. I have a beer with him. He has made me a believer in Bob's Rule.

THE BASS QUEEN'S LAST BASS
OF THE SEASON

My wife, The Bass Queen, is in great turmoil. It is a Sunday morning in the middle of October. The Bass Queen had just celebrated her birthday a couple of days earlier and she considered this weekend part of her birthday.

On Saturday we had gone to an art fair at a small town on the Mississippi River. A cold, mean blustery wind came off the river. We were bundled up in several layers of clothes as we walked around the tents that covered the displays of art work. We saw a lot of people wearing winter coats, stocking caps pulled over their ears and hands in gloves, clutching steaming cups of coffee and hot chocolate.

On the way back home we stopped at a landing on the river and talked to a father and son, who had just came off the water and were getting their boat and trailer ready for the drive home. They had not caught a fish and saw very few people around them catch fish.

"I think we were hurt by this cold front that blew in," the father said to us, referring to the last several days of nasty weather that we had been having.

But Sunday is a different day. The wind had dropped and the sun danced brightly off colored trees. When I get the newspapers from the mail box it felt warm and pleasant outside. This sudden and glorious change in weather awakened a desire with The Bass Queen to go fishing.

By her own admission, The Bass Queen is a fair weather fisherperson. Once the cool days of fall arrive she usually hangs up her spinning rods for the year. But this day was begging us to go fishing. There is a sense of urgency to this day. By next weekend it, likely, would be too cold for her to want to go fishing and she knew that this would be her last day of the season.

She is tormented by the thought of getting skunked and not catching any fish. It has been several years since The Bass Queen has been skunked and she takes great pride in that. But this day has all the potential for getting skunked. Air and water temperatures have been dropping daily and this is the first good day after a cold front had wrecked havoc. Plus it is late in the season and bass are getting sluggish by this time. Getting skunked on her birthday weekend and the last day of her season would be more than she could handle. The Bass Queen takes getting skunked very personal.

But the beauty and warmth of the day wins her over and she says, "Let's go fishing." I load the boat with bass gear and hook it up to the van and we are off. We go to Lake X. It is The Bass Queen's favorite lake.

As we drive to the lake she is wracked with doubts.

"What if I get skunked?" She asks.

"You won't," I assure her. "You have never been skunked at Lake X."

On the first point that we fish I catch a small bass. The Bass Queen gets nothing.

"This could be the day," she says. "I could get skunked."

"You must have faith," I tell her.

"No," she says. "I must have fish."

We fish a long a rocky bank and then another point and I catch another fish.

"This is not looking good," The Bass Queen says.

"We just started," I tell her. A few moments later I catch another bass.

"I am doomed," The Bass Queen announces. I try to be reassuring but I see that it is not working real well.

We move into a shallow bay. We occasionally catch some fish in this bay but usually we do not start to pick up many fish until we hit the point at the far end of the bay. I thought we would just fish quickly through this bay to get to the point. I am now starting to get anxious. The Bass Queen has to catch a fish soon.

I hear her yell and I look up to see her spinning rod doubled over. I quickly bring in my rod, drop it on the floor of the boat and get ready to help her land the fish. It looks to be a big fish by the way her spinning rod has doubled over and the way the fish keeps pulling away. Finally I see the fish in the water and it is indeed a good fish. Now I am really getting anxious. She has to get this fish. She gets the fish alongside the boat and as I reach down to grab the fish, I keep saying to myself, "Don't mess this up." I grab the line, stick my thumb in the fish's mouth, clamp down, and hoist the fish into the boat.

The Bass Queen is all smiles now. I measure the fish and it is nineteen inches long and weights four and a half pounds.

"Thank you." She says to the fish as she slides it back into the water.

It was not the last fish that she would catch that day, as she catches another three of four smaller fish by the time we quit. But it is the one that she still remembers. It was the fish that insured she would not be skunked on her last day of the season on her birthday weekend.

THE END OF THE SEASON

The fishing season ends for me when I finally put the boat away for the winter. This usually happens sometime in early December. But up until that point I try to squeeze in as many fishing trips that I can get out of those few remaining days of decent weather in late November and early December.

I can reasonably expect to be on the river the weekend before Thanksgiving. Sometimes it is a bit chilly that time of year but the Mississippi River is still open and the landings aren't too icy so that I can still get the boat on and off the water.

On this last year my son-in-law, Damien, and I fished on the Saturday before Thanksgiving and on Sunday, my old army buddy and fishing pal, Doug, and I went fishing. This weekend also coincides with the opening of the Wisconsin gun season for deer. There are fewer boats on the water than I had seen earlier in the month so apparently the start of the deer hunting season has taken a lot of fishermen off the water.

For walleyes and sauger, the fish hit surprisingly hard and with the cold water they seemed unusually frisky. The days are gray and windy and strings of geese are etched against the swirling dark November skies. Eagles cavorted overhead.

It is two good days of fishing but I am still holding out for a couple of more days of fishing. The Monday before Thanksgiving I clean out the garage. I pull the boat out into the driveway and wash it down. The fact that it is still warm enough to wash the boat gives me hope that the weather will stay mild enough to get back on the water yet. Bags of cans go to the recycle center.

The lawn furniture finally comes in from the deck and is piled on one side of the garage. There is still a fairly substantial pile of assorted boxes with stuff in it that I leave in the middle of the garage to be stored later in the boat. There is no room to bring in my wife's SUV yet with no place to put the boxes and I hope to get the boat out and still go fishing.

Thanksgiving has wonderful weather and throughout the weekend I am outside in shirt sleeves. I have family responsibilities to attend to through the long Thanksgiving weekend but I have hopes for the following weekend. Even though now it will be into December.

Thanksgiving is over and I still have plans to go fishing. I have made calls to several people who have agreed that possibly we can still get on the river. The first weekend in December is set. But suddenly the weather turns bad and the temperatures drop. It gets cold and the lakes begin to freeze over. Late in the week I get a call from one buddy. It is supposed to be in the single digits on Saturday and even colder on Sunday. He backs out. My son, Todd, is still up for it and we choose Saturday as our day to go since it is supposed to be the warmest day of the weekend.

Saturday morning it is only thirteen degrees as we drive to the river. It is cold but it will be the last day of fishing for the year so we got to go. My wife, The Bass Queen, thinks I am nuts. I'm sure my son thinks I am nuts too but still agrees to go. On the water I see only three other boats. I guess that there are a couple of other nuts besides me. A cold wind blows down the river. The line freezes in the rod guides. The outside of the boat is incrusted in ice. We last two hours and call it quits. We caught four sauger so at least we weren't skunked.

Two days later the temperatures plummet down to zero at night and it looks like winter has a lock on the weather until spring. The Bass Queen tells me she wants to get her SUV in the garage so she won't have to scrape the windows in the morning when she goes to work. The next morning after she goes to work, I jockey the boat as far to the side of the garage where all the deck furniture and lawn mowers and tools are lined up. I take all the boxes of stuff that has been sitting on the garage floor and pile that in the boat. The spare seat for my van gets slid on top of the back casting deck. The boat will now and for the rest of the winter become a repository for all sorts of junk. I ask the boat to forgive me. I tell it that it will only be about a hundred days or so before we can get back on the river.

The Bass Queen now has room to get her SUV in the garage. She is very happy with that. The fishing season is finally over and the boat is in an incapacitated state until that magical day in spring when I can finally get back on the river again.

Christmas is rapidly approaching. There is not much of the year left. But suddenly after the boat is piled high with assorted stuff and jammed into the side of the garage the weather turns warm. It becomes almost balmy. I am tempted but I know that as soon as I unload the boat to get it out, the temperatures will nose dive back to zero. I guess that I will just have to wait until spring.

ON A WINTER'S DAY

It is snowing. This is not mere snow flurries. This is a blizzard and not just any blizzard. This is the biggest snowfall of the winter and with less than a month of winter remaining; it is looking like this might be the last one of the season. The weather people on television have been talking non stop about this storm for the last two days so there is much hysteria.

Yesterday the grocery store took a beating as worried people, expecting the worse that the televised panic could generate, raided the grocery stores. To get ready for the storm I checked the liquor and beer supply. We have enough to get us through a fairly large weather catastrophe. We have lots of food in the house and a bunch of firewood stacked outside the back door. We were ready to let the blizzard begin.

And then it hit. It started with a light snow in the morning and changed to rain; just enough to put a light coat of ice over everything and make going anywhere treacherous. Then the wind picked up and it started to snow again. By afternoon the wind was howling around the house, tearing at the pine grove in our back yard, and blowing clouds of powdery snow across the lawn. It had all the signs of the worst snow storm of the winter or even possibly the last couple of winters. It was going to be one heck of a blizzard.

One of the nice things about being a writer is that I can write anytime and I always have a story that I could work on. Because I write I also read and I have a large collection of books. But on this winter day I don't feel like starting on another story or reading any of the four books that I have started and are sitting on the table next to my chair in the family room. Instead I go down to the Supply Room which is my name for the basement. I have a couple of chores with some fishing tackle that I have been meaning to get to and this winter's day seems like the best time to do that.

I have several small boxes and a couple of bags of spinners that I have been meaning to sort through and consolidate in one plastic box. Plus I have been meaning, for some time, to go though the tackle box I take to Canada. I can't think of better projects while a blizzard is raging outside.

I pour myself a cup of coffee and dump the spinners on the dining room table, spreading them out in front of me. As I sort through them, grouping like spinners together and depositing them in a larger plastic box. I remind myself that I need to use more in-line spinners next fishing season. I have a group of large, bright spinners that I had used for stripers when I lived in Alabama and I think that they would work well on white bass here.

There is another batch of white, pink and silver spinners that I had used on white bass one late fall day on a lake near to my home in Hudson, Wisconsin. We just slammed white bass that day and at times caught fish on every other cast. Interesting enough, although I have gone back to the lake several more times since that day, I never caught white bass like that again. Using that same spinner one late spring day in May on the Fox River near Oshkosh, Wisconsin, my wife, the Bass Queen, and I ran into another large school of white bass and in less than a couple of hours we had caught and released over forty white bass.

There is another group of large, flashy spinners that I had used for northerns in Canada. That prompted me to open up the tackle box I take to Canada. I had intended to take some things out of it and I do that but then I think I just might need that up there. When you have been dropped off by float plane at a wilderness outpost cabin for five days you just can't race down to the local sport shop to get something if you don't have it. So I put most of the things I have taken out of it back in the box. Although I know that I will probably never really need it, I will have it if I do.

The wind blasts snow against the large glass porch door behind me but winter is no longer my concern. In my mind it is summer and I am in Canada and warm breezes rustle through the pine trees and wash waves against the rocky shoreline and I am in a boat, catching fish. Winter has no hold on me. The memories take over and I am thinking about fishing and warm summer days and the gentle rock of the boat and seeing a fish erupt on the surface of the water. Even though I am doing more reminiscing, I still get my projects done and take all of the equipment back to the Supply Room.

Then later that night when the wind is still howling and the snow is pounding the sides of the house, I take out perch fillets from fish that I caught a couple of weeks earlier in another blizzard while fishing Devils Lake in North Dakota. The fillets are dipped in egg wash and rolled in bread crumbs and dropped in hot oil. The smell of fish frying fills the kitchen and again I am transported, in my mind, back to summer days where the fish are hitting and the living is easy and of fish fries in the back yard.

Winter be damned. I am thinking of spring and fishing. I won't even worry about blowing out the driveway until maybe tomorrow.

BLOWING OUT THE SNOW

It is cold and windy and it has been snowing for two days. This is the second blizzard that we had in a week. This is getting to be a bit annoying. In five days I will be in Mexico, sitting on a sandy beach with warm ocean breezes and many rum drinks. Why couldn't these blizzards have held off for a few more days until after I left?

It seems that every day for the last week I have been cranking up the snow blower. Today it is no different. I am standing in the garage pulling The Machine, my name for the snow blower, out of its spot where I sandwiched it in between the bow of the boat and the wall of the garage. Will the boat ever see open water again or will it snow forever?

I drag The Machine out into the driveway and fill it with gas. Snow swirls around me as I am clutching the gas can trying not to spill gas all over the top of The Machine. Is it me or what, but do all six gallon cans of gas seem to weigh a ton and are cumbersome to pour? And why do all small engines have such small gas caps that make it almost impossible to pour gas into it without spilling gas? These are some of the mysteries of life that perplex me at this moment as the gas inevitably runs over.

I am rewarded by the rumble of the engine as The Machine comes to life with the electric start. I adjust the throttle until the engine stops sputtering and is now running smoothly.

Looking at the driveway I see where I have a foot of snow. It is still snowing and will continue through the night. I could just let it go until tomorrow but by then who knows how much I will have. Getting it done now will make it easier tomorrow to clean it up once the storm is over.

My driveway is not that long but it does go up a small hill where it attaches to the road. When I am on the bottom part of the hill I am fairly well out of the wind but when I hit the top of the hill the wind gets me then and I see the wind drifting sheets of snow over the top of the driveway.

I start the first pass with The Machine. As I hit the top, the wind blows the snow back towards me covering me in a white cloud of snow. One of the other mysteries is that no matter which direction I try to blow the snow the wind still blows it back towards me. Even when I try to blow it in the same direction the wind is blowing it always seem to get blown back into my face. It is another one of the great snow blowing mysteries that I wonder about when I am blowing out the driveway.

After the third pass on the driveway, the snow has blown down both the front and back of my jacket. My black jacket is now white and I have snow piling up on the top of my hat. Snow has splattered against my cheeks and I have a slush buildup on my glasses. I can not see through the glasses any longer so I have to take them off and put them in a pocket.

I know that there will be a day and, it is only a couple of months away, when I will be sitting in my boat with warm spring winds and catching fish. So perhaps these blizzards are just a small price that I have to pay to get me from the end of one fishing season to the start of another.

As I am thinking about my lakes I remember that last fall they were as low as I have seen them in the last ten years. I had remarked, last fall, that we needed snow this winter to fill those lakes with water and bring the water tables back up.

So again, if these blizzards we are now getting bring the water back up in my favorite lakes then it also is a small price to pay. The wind is still blowing snow down the front and back of my jacket and slaps me in the face with its cold, icy sting but knowing that this snow is helping my lakes stay healthy makes me feel better.

The Machine and I make the last run down the driveway. It is done for now. I brush off The Machine before I slip it between the bow of the boat and the wall of the garage. I charge inside, dropping clothing as I run for the bathroom.

I immerse myself into a tub of hot water and feel the chill begin to slip away. My wife, the Bass Queen, brings me a hot toddy. It is hot tea, with lemon and honey and a shot of bourbon. I never knew that tea could taste that good.

In five days I will be in Mexico and I won't care about blowing out the driveway. But I am happy for the snow right now. My lakes need it.

THE MAGIC ROD

It is a magical rod and reel combination. It is something that just got thrown together over the years but has yielded the most unusual results. It is certainly not a very pretty rod considering I have a number of hand made rods. Nor is it very expensive. In fact both the rod and reel never cost me a cent. It is certainly not the best rod and reel that I own. In fact most people would think of it as junk.

I do not use it often and for the most part it just sits in the Supply Room, that I call the basement. But this rod and reel combo, from such modest origins, has provided me two most extraordinary fishing experiences.

Originally, I got the rod when I was last stationed in Germany in the late 1980s on my last overseas tour with the Army. I was a member of the Heidelberg Rod and Gun Club and at one of the monthly meetings I won the rod during a drawing. It was nothing spectacular. It was a red, two piece, six foot spinning carbon composite rod with a black foam handle made in Germany. It seemed to be a light sensitive rod.

Initially I had it matched with a couple of different reels. It accompanied me often to Canada and it was good for fishing jigs. I had leant it to one of my fishing buddies one year in Canada and he liked it well enough that he threatened to steal it if I wasn't careful.

But it didn't become magical until I put an old black Abu Garcia Cardinal C4 reel with it. A few months after my father passed away, my mother asked my brother and I to go through his fishing equipment, split it up and take what we wanted. I spied that old reel and, although it probably was twenty years old, I felt for some reason that it would be the perfect reel for that red German spinning rod.

The reel needed some work and a small plate across the bail spring was missing. I have a buddy of mine that does reel repair and I sent it to him. He cleaned it up and replaced the plate. After that I noticed that it still made some funny noises when cranking the reel so it probably would not be the best for casting but I thought it would make a fine reel for vertical jigging.

This is when it became magical.

On the next trip to Canada I took it along. One afternoon my son-in-law, Brian, and I were fishing the mouth of a river that emptied into the lake our cabin was on. I was using a jig with a three inch chartreuse grub. I dropped the jig to the bottom and was bouncing it off the rocks.

I felt a sharp strike and when I set the hook, the fish came up about a foot and a half and then just stopped. I could not get it to budge further. Slowly and deliberately the fish took off as the drag on the reel gave out the line. I yelled to Brian that I had a big fish and I heard noises in the boat as he was moving things to get the net. I turned the fish and was getting some line back when it took off in a spurt of speed. I turned the fish again and finally after a tug of war that lasted a few moments I had the fish under the boat. I would lift the fish up and then it would sink back down again.

We were anxious to see this fish. I was winning the battle. For every foot and a half that I was getting the fish up it would only dive about a foot, so I was winning by inches. The fish was getting closer to the boat but we still could not see it. I lifted the rod and then cranked on the reel as I dropped the rod. One or two more times and we would be able to see the fish. Then it was alongside the boat and when I looked over I saw my jig in the mouth of a twenty two inch northern pike with another thirty two inch northern that had latched onto the northern that had it the jig. I had seen northern pike attack fish that I had on the line before but never one that stayed with it all the way to the boat.

But the magic did not stop there. This last spring I had a new jig I wanted to try while fishing for walleyes on the Mississippi River. So I grabbed that rod in the morning before I left and tied on the jig. My buddy Scott asked me where I got that old rod from when I pulled it out of the rod locker. We had not fished for more than five minutes when I felt a fish slam into it. The fish hit so hard that there was no setting the hook. The fish tore off and it felt like I just tied onto the trailer hitch of a speeding truck. The drag crunched away as the fish took off line.

Although I stopped the run I could not get the fish any closer as it stubbornly held to the bottom just pulling against the rod. Finally I began to gain some line and I could feel the fish grudgingly get closer. By this time Scott was standing next to me with the net and we both were peering into the dirty river water trying to see what kind of fish I had. We expected to see a big catfish. We saw the shadow in the water and I pulled back again to where we could finally see the fish. It was about a fifteen pound paddle fish. In over half a century of fishing, I had never caught one before.

The magic had continued. I am looking forward to the next time when I use that rod and reel. I wonder what magic still awaits me.

HELPING EACH OTHER

We were talking fishing. Our boats were alongside each other floating on one of our favorite lakes. Our friend Jerry was in one boat and The Bass Queen and I were in our boat. It had been a busy and hectic early season so far and we had not seen Jerry for some time. We had lots to catch up on. Where had we been fishing? How was the season going? We asked about his father now in a nursing home and we told him about our son getting married in Las Vegas.

As we talked dark, ugly bruised storm clouds began to build behind us in the west. This storm had been coming for some time and in the last hour we had seen a bright, sunny, hot early summer day slowly dissolve into a gray layered sky with cooler temperatures.

There was a rumble of thunder and a flash of lightening. The Bass Queen said that was enough. We had to go in; a storm was coming on fast. Jerry said he thought he might try to fish through it. We headed to the landing.

The lake was dead, eerie calm as we approached the dock at the landing. Another boat was blocking the landing as two fishermen were hooking up their straps. They could see that the storm was rapidly moving in and they said that they would move their boat.

I jumped onto the dock as The Bass Queen beached the boat next to the dock leaving the side next to the landing open. I hurried to get the van and within the couple of minutes it took me to walk to the parking lot and drive the van down to the landing the wind struck. It howled across the water, whipping the water into whitecaps and as I drove a tree branch snapped off a tree blowing onto the road.

Jerry must have thought better of it and his boat was pulled up on the shore on the other side of the landing. The wind had spun our boat around and The Bass Queen was struggling to hold onto it. Jerry was standing next to her on the dock and they both were pulling on the bow line.

I quickly backed the trailer into the water and jumped out of the van, running up on the dock. I jumped into the boat and was quickly trying to start the motor. It finally caught and I threw the throttle into reverse trying to back the boat off shore. Finally it pulled loose and I ran it up on the trailer. By now the rain started to pound down. Jerry waded out into the water and hooking up the winch rope and safety chain, he cranked the boat up the rest of the way onto the trailer.

As The Bass Queen drove the van, dragging me and the boat out of the water, she yelled for Jerry to get in and we would drop him off at his truck in the parking lot. Once Jerry got into his truck, we followed him back to the landing. Jerry backed his trailer into the water and then drove his boat off the shore and onto his trailer where I was standing to hook his winch up for him. As I was cranking his boat on the trailer, another boat came motoring up to the landing. It had a young family in it; a father, mother and young son. Fear was written on the young boy's face and the mother was doing her best not to frighten him any more but you could see that she was clearly anxious.

The father beached the boat and he and the young son raced to the parking lot to get their truck and trailer. I was lashing down the last straps on my boat when the father was trying to back the trailer into the landing. The trailer jack knifed and he was trying to straighten it out but was having a tough time of it. I ran down and pulled the trailer straight for him, telling him to back it in.

He jumped out of his truck and got into his boat, driving it around the dock and tried to run it up on the trailer. He had a couple of small bunks on the trailer but the current had twisted them. I waded out and pushed them back into position but that was little help as the wind tore at the boat and continued to wash it off the trailer. He got out of the boat and we pulled the boat on the trailer by hand but the waves were still pushing the boat off the trailer as he tried to drive it out of the landing.

The rain was pounding down. I waded out into the water and pushing the boat back on the trailer. He drove his truck, inching out of the landing and I pushed against the boat on the trailer as I walked alongside. The trailer cleared the water and the boat was only slightly askew. I walked behind him until he stopped and we just lifted the back of the boat up and placed it squarely on the trailer.

I walked back to the van. My t-shirt was soaked, clinging to my wet skin. When I slid into the van The Bass Queen handed me a sweatshirt and I pulled off the wet shirt and gratefully slipped into the dry one. As we drove past the young family the father was lashing the boat down and his wife waved to us and yelled her thanks.

As we drive along the road, dodging around the tree branches that had been blown down, I realized that people, even complete strangers, have to pull together in times of need to help each other. That is what humanity is all about.

A CATFISH EXPERIENCE

At first I thought I was snagged. This thought only lasted for a second or two though, once I could feel the thumping of a fish against the rod. My spinning rod was bent in half.

"This is a fish," I said to my fishing buddy Doug. "Whatever it is, it is big."

The fish was pulling against the rod and reel and I could feel line beginning to peel off the drag. The fish stayed deep and continued to pull away. It acted as if my spinning rod was just a mere irritant. It slowly and methodically moved off seeming unhindered by my doubled over spinning rod.

Doug had brought in his spinning rod and was standing next to me with the net.

I could not budge the fish. It stayed on the bottom and I could feel it move off, but I could not get it to stir an inch closer to the boat. I was just holding on and the fish was drifting down river with the current with us following in the boat.

The fish stayed deep and occasionally the drag would give off more line. If it had not been for the fact that I could feel the fish moving below me it could have been a snag. But this was alive and moving.

It was at least five minutes and I still had not gotten the fish to budge from the bottom. Finally I could feel it move and I got a couple of cranks on the reel but then the fish just stopped. I could not get it to come any closer and my spinning rod and eight pound test line was straining as much I thought it could bear.

"Must be a big catfish or sturgeon," Doug said. Doug and I have both seen these big fish on the Mississippi River before and we both had said that you will never know what you will catch on the Mississippi.

The fish pulled away and my drag seemed to do nothing to stop it. The fish would stop and I would pull back, gaining a couple of yards of line and then the fish would just simply pull away taking whatever line I had retrieved back off the reel.

At one point I was holding the spinning rod with both hands. I could feel the muscles tighten in my arm and shoulder. I have had fish in salt water do this to me but never in fresh water.

Finally I began to start getting the fish closer to the boat. Doug and I both were peering intently into the dirty, dingy Mississippi water anxiously trying to get a glimpse of the fish.

There was a swirl still deep below the water and I could feel the fish getting closer. I was pulling back on the spinning rod while holding the spool so that it would not give out line and would reel quickly when I dropped the rod tip to gain line. I pulled back trying to move the fish closer again. The last time I had to pump a fishing rod like this to gain line was four months earlier when I caught a six foot shark off Key West, Florida.

Another foot or two and we would be able to see the fish. I probably was forcing the fish but I really wanted to see what I had. Then it finally was there. It was a large brown shape in the muddy water and as it came closer to the boat it looked prehistoric. It was a flathead catfish and it looked huge. It looked like it could swallow my entire arm.

"We can forget the net," Doug said. Although my net was good sized there was no way that fish was going to fit in it. The fish turned and moved away, pulling line off the reel and disappearing back into the murky water. The line just kept peeling off the reel and it seemed as if all the line I had gained in the last fifteen of twenty minutes was lost again.

I pulled back and the fish stopped but it would not move an inch. It stayed deep and I could feel the fish thumping against the rod. I was back to holding the spinning rod with both hands and my arm was aching.

I felt I was starting all over again and the minutes ticked off as I would get a yard or two of line back. We seesawed back and forth but finally the fish was getting closer. Doug got the neoprene gloves out from under the front deck and was waiting.

Now finally the fish was getting close enough to once again see it in the water but each time I got it close enough for Doug to grab, the fish would pull away. Doug finally had the fish but it slipped out of his hands. I brought the fish back and Doug grabbed it again and pulled it over the gunnels of the boat. I grabbed Doug and we both slid the fish into the boat.

The fish was over four feet long and about a foot and half across the head. It would take both hands to hold the fish while Doug took a couple of quick photos. I slid it back into the water and it slowly moved away disappearing into the dirty spring water of the Mississippi River.

MY SECRET FISHING SPOT

I found it all by myself and it belonged to me. Anyone that fishes wants their very own secret fishing spot that is just theirs and where you can always catch fish. It has not been often in my life that I have had a secret fishing spot but I did once when I was a boy.

I lived only about a quarter of a mile from Lake Winnebago in eastern Wisconsin and so from early childhood on I had been prowling along the lake shores close to my home. Straight down from my house there was a large shallow bay with a fire lane that went into the water. The fire lane was a narrow strip of public land that some people occasionally used as a boat launch. There was a large field next to the fire lane that we kids just assumed was for us and we played there. On the lake front of this field was a sandy beach where we swam. It made for great lazy, summer afternoons. I remember once that a bunch of us, both guys and girls, in a pre-puberty burst of the risqué went skinny dipping.

Our sandy swimming hole was at the back of the bay and the shoreline turned east. On the southern end of the bay where the large field and sandy beach ended there was a dark and, to our young minds, a very mysterious woods. I had explored these woods with a sense of youthful daring and found a small, dilapidated cabin that probably was not much larger than an old ice house. Perhaps at one time that was what it actually was. This discovery only added to the mystique of these woods.

No one often ventured into or even near the woods. The sandy beach ran out right about where the woods began and the shore line and bottom became rocky. Not good for swimming. Eventually our field became built up and two or three large homes were placed there. The new people were not pleased about our swimming in that bay and did their best to discourage us.

But the woods and its mystery remained. About this time I began to lose interest in the water for swimming purposes and began to look at it from a fishermen's perspective. The bay certainly was too shallow and sandy for fishing but that wooded area was different. The water was a little deeper there; the rocks might hold fish and no one else went there. I had become a student of Sports Afield and other outdoor magazines. I had read a number of stories about how bait fish will migrate from deeper water to shallow water as the sun goes down and, of course, the game fish will follow them. Along the shoreline in my mysterious little woods there was a small rocky point, probably only about six or eight feet long that protruded out into the lake. I just thought that it might be a place that would have fish on a summers evening.

So one night I got on my bike and peddled down there. I hid the bike in a ditch and cut through the woods with my waders over my shoulder and my spinning rod in hand. Once I got to the little mini point, I pulled off my shoes, slipped on the waders and waded out into the water. In those days the only bait I ever used was a Johnson Silver minnow and in addition to the one attached to the line I had another one or two in my shirt pocket.

I waded out into the water to about my waist and started to cast. Within a few minutes I felt a jolt on the end of my line. The fight was spectacular and the fish rocketed out of the water. When I finally got it in I found that it was a nice sized smallmouth bass. A little while later, I caught another smallmouth and then a white bass and then just before it was totally dark I lost another fish that I never saw.

Once it was too dark to see where I was casting, I quit. I waded back to shore, peeled of my waders and put my shoes back on. With a flashlight probing into the fearful darkness I retraced my steps, dragging the stringer of fish, back to the bike. I will admit that I was a bit spooked by the time I got back to the bike and began to ride home. But I also felt very satisfied. I had found this spot and I had done it all by myself.

This became my secret spot. I shared it with no one else except my boyhood buddy, Gary. I remember one evening that he and I fished it and he caught a twenty two inch walleye and I caught a twenty four inch northern. For young teen boys they were huge trophies.

For the next three years or so before we discovered cars and girls, Gary and I or sometimes just I would go to this secret spot. We never caught a lot of fish there but we always seemed to catch some fish. That is all that a young fisherman really needs. It was always a little spooky walking back to our bikes through the woods in the dark but it never stopped us from going back.

That was forty years ago and that spooky, mysterious woods has disappeared. Someone finally took out a bunch of trees and built homes there. But once, it was my secret spot and I remember warm, summer nights catching fish there and the joy of having a secret spot that only I and my buddy knew. And I found it all by myself.

THE WORLDS WORST DRESSED
OUTDOOR WRITER

I had just returned from Cozumel, Mexico where in addition to spending most of my time sitting on the beach and drinking rum drinks I had gone fishing for bonefish. I was showing my buddy, Doug, my fishing photos.

"Nice fish," he said.

"What else do you see there?" I asked.

"Nice Packer hat." Doug and I both are Packer fans.

"What else?" I persisted.

He looked hard at the photos for a minute or two.

"I can't believe it," he finally said. "You are not wearing a t-shirt."

In the photo I was holding a two pound bonefish and wearing, in addition to my Packer hat, a nylon pair of shorts and one of those fancy nylon short sleeve fishing shirts with lots of pockets. I looked like a real fisherman and a bona fide outdoor writer.

I will confess to dressing casual. My wife, the Bass Queen, may even call it haphazard. I have never seen a need to get dressed up to go fishing. If I am going to be spending the day in the boat I want to be comfortable. That means shorts and a t-shirt for most of the summer.

Unfortunately, I have a number of my friends that dress very fashionably when they go fishing. When I am sitting in the same boat with them I feel like I am sitting in church next to a guy in a suit and I am wearing a bowling team shirt.

The Bass Queen has done her best to get me dressed up. When we were dating my mother told me later she knew I must be seeing someone because my selection of t-shirts greatly improved. The Bass Queen has made an effort. Every year for Christmas she gets me several new t-shirts with a fishing theme to them. I call them my "go to church" shirts. The shirts from the year before get added to the rest of my shirts and then become my fishing shirts.

Some of these shirts have sentimental value to them and others have wonderful pictures of bass jumping out of the water or neat fishing sayings on them. I just hate to get rid of them just because they have a hole in them or a stain on the front. The Bass Queen does not understand that. Even some of my fishing buddies do not understand that.

My choice of fashion does not go well when I am fishing with some of my more fashionably dressed fishing partners. I regularly run into one buddy, Jerry, who always dresses impeccably. He is always color coordinated and his fishing shirts look like they are pressed. Although we are in different boats I think he is embarrassed to be on the same lake with me.

My buddy Doug is also a well dressed fisherman. He always looks like he has stepped out of one of those outdoor catalogs with just the right shirt and shorts or pants.

Since hanging around Doug and Jerry it has occurred to me that as an outdoor writer I need to upgrade my fishing wardrobe. So I went out and bought several of those fancy nylon fishing shirts with all the pockets. I have not quite figured out why we need to have that many pockets. It is just too easy to lose stuff in all those pockets. None of my t-shirts had pockets and I got along just fine.

So on a recent fishing trip with Doug, every morning after we ate breakfast, we both went into our bedrooms and got into our formal wear. When I showed The Bass Queen the photos from our fishing she was impressed.

"You were even color coordinated," she gushed.

I used to have one ally, my fishing buddy Scott. When I first me him, outside of the shirts he wore at work, everything else he wore were sleeveless t-shirts. With the exception of his work shirts I didn't think that he even owned a shirt with sleeves.

But then he started dating a girl, named Sara and they just got married a couple of months ago. I noticed that shortly after they started dating that he started wearing shirts with sleeves even when he went fishing. Then came the fancy fishing shirts; I could see the handwriting on the wall. I was losing my ally.

Just a couple of weeks ago The Bass Queen and I saw them while we were out fishing. Scott was wearing a stylish pair of nylon pants and a white nylon fishing shirt. He looked positively dapper.

I knew it right then. It was over for me. I was going to have to buy some more fishing shirts. I guess that I will just have to get over all those pockets. Besides, we outdoor writers need to be looking good.

TOOLS OF THE TRADE

When The Bass Queen and I stopped by to see our friends, Kurt and Penny, while we were back recently in our hometown of Oshkosh, Wisconsin, I found Kurt in the garage. He had his hands in the engine of a 1968 Porsche 912. By trade, Kurt is a truck tester for a large truck manufacturing company but cars are his passion. A few years ago Kurt and his son got into the stock car racing business. Now that the stock car racing is over, he bought this Porsche as his toy car. It is a beautiful car with a bright red body, new leather seats and a motor for Kurt to play with.

On this particular Saturday afternoon, Kurt was trying to pull off a starter in preparation to pull the motor. Not only was he up to his elbows in the motor but he was muttering very unpleasant things about the people who designed this particular model of Porsche.

"This should have been a twenty minute job," Kurt was saying. "But I have spent all afternoon at it and there is hardly any way to get to this nut" he continued, stabbing a finger at a photograph in his mechanics book. Although I have no experience in auto mechanics, I could see his predicament. The bolt had to be loosened from the bottom but the top of the nut had to be secured from the top of the motor to keep it from slipping. It looked like it certainly would take two people to do this so I volunteered to assist.

With a mirror and a flashlight we found the nut and he was able to get a wrench on it. Once that was done I held the wrench tight while Kurt crawled under the Porsche and finally was able to loosen the nut and pull out the starter. With the starter loose, Kurt decided to call it a day with his toy car and it was late enough in the afternoon that we decided to meet our wives back at the house for cocktail hour.

As Kurt was cleaning up his tools and laying them out in his garage work bench he told me that he had at least four set of tools. He had his tool box at work, a set of tools on hooks on the garage wall and on the bench in the garage. He had another set of tools in the basement of the house so that he did not have to race out to the garage every time he needed a tool and another box of tools he took when he and his son went to the race track.

Now it seems to me that for a man who makes his living working on trucks and plays with cars in his spare time, that it is reasonable and necessary for him to have several sets of tools. I understand this completely.

I feel this way about fishing equipment. In my basement, that I call the Supply Room, I have over a hundred rod and reel combinations. For someone who fishes a lot and writes about fishing this is not particularly excessive. These are tools. Because I fish for just about everything, there are different rod and reel combos for different fish and different fishing situations. You are going to need different tools. Once we had a crew replacing the siding on our house and the foreman saw the Supply Room and mentioned to me that I had a lot of rod and reels. When I told them that they were like tools to me he shook his in understanding, telling me that he had at least six hammers in his truck.

All of the rods are stored in rod racks that sit on the Supply Room floor. I am predominately a bass fisherman so the biggest rod rack has about fifteen bass fishing rods. Those include The Bass Queen's rods. She would not be The Bass Queen if she did not have her own rods.

Another rack has about ten rods that I use only for walleye fishing. Half of them are heavier rods that I use for heavier baits on the Mississippi River in the early spring and late fall. The rest are lighter rods for lighter baits that I use in lakes during the regular fishing season. Now someone could make the argument that I could use the bass rods for walleye fishing as well, but that would not be convenient.

Then I have one rack that has light spinning rods and fly rods for trout fishing. Another rack has ultralight spinning rods for panfish and another rack has heavy casting rods for muskie fishing. Obviously you can't use a muskie rod for panfish or a panfish rod for muskies. Different tools are needed.

I then have a rack of rods that are old fiberglass rods with old Mitchell 300 reels. I have found them to be the ideal trolling combo. Another rack has less expensive rods and reels that I use when I go to the Boundary Waters or Canada. Equipment takes such a beating there that I would hate to wreck one of the better rods there. One year in the Boundary Waters two of the guys in our group rolled over a canoe and lost all of their fishing equipment. No need to lose good tools there. I have another rack with rods that I reserve for the guests that fish at my house and one last rack with some various spare rod and reel combos.

These are tools of the trade. Occasionally the Bass Queen will take another wife down to show her the Supply

Room. The other wife always comes back upstairs shaking her head and gives her husband a look that says "don't even think about it." One lady did say that it did look nicely organized.

Regardless of what others might think, any mechanic can tell you that you can never have too many tools.

HOMEGROWN FISH FRY

The family garden is slowly disappearing from the American landscape. It follows a number of other landmarks such as the family dinner time from the way of life that I remember from my days growing up in the 1950s and 60s. During my boyhood, the family dinner time and family garden was an institution of the middle class American way of life.

In those days my father had a huge garden in our back yard. We lived on a full acre in the country. It was a good place to raise kids and a garden.

He seemed to have a little bit of everything. Tomatoes, sweet corn, cucumbers, potatoes, onions and beans were staples of his garden. Then he had squash and he experimented with a number of varieties and even a couple of pumpkin plants that provided our jack-o-lanterns at Halloween. He had strawberries and they were the largest that I have ever seen. For a number of years he tried lettuce, peas, asparagus and a number of other things.

In the spring he would turn over the dark ground with a rototiller and meticulously plant his crops by hand. On hot summer evenings I can vividly remember my father dragging the water hose out to the garden to water. For plants that were too far from the stretched hose to reach, he would fill buckets of water to carry to them. He would spend hours contently weeding his garden when he came home after work. Then as each crop reached its season he would pick them.

Although we lived in the country I never remember my father complaining about animals getting into his garden. A few rabbits would get into the garden now and then but Father never felt that he was competing with them. I suppose he felt that there was enough to go around for everyone. Sometimes in the early morning or late evening an occasional deer would wander into Father's garden from the woods behind our acre. There were not many of them in those days so it was always a pleasant surprise to see them and Father and our whole family took joy in watching them. If they got a few vegetables it was a fair trade off to just see them, as far as my father was concerned.

With exceptions of the strawberries that began in mid June and squash and pumpkins that would be due in fall, everything else in the garden ripened in the late summer. August was a particularly busy time with the garden. There were lots of vegetables to harvest.

For my mother this was an especially busy time. She would be canning and freezing all the stuff that came in from the garden. She made the best strawberry jam I have ever had. We had a separate room in the basement that we called the root cellar where all the jars of garden stuff she canned would be stored, waiting to be eaten during the cold days of winter. Years later, in my late teen years, she would allow me to share that room as a dark room when I began to process my own photos.

My mother is a wonderful cook and it was also during the late summer harvesting time that she would make many of the things fresh from the garden for the family dinner. My parents took a great deal of pride in this. My father growing and harvesting and my mother cooking and canning.

I remember one meal in particular. I had caught a bunch of fish. I do not remember exactly what type of fish that they were but they probably were yellow perch and bluegills. I cleaned the fish and buried the guts in the garden. Over the years of my youth I fertilized that garden often with fish guts.

A day or two later my mother made those fish for dinner. She pan fried them in butter until the edges turned crispy brown. We had boiled potatoes and corn on the cob and green beans all with melted butter. Women cooked a lot with butter in those days. We had tomatoes from the garden sprinkled with salt. They also used a lot of salt in those days. And for dessert we had strawberries in cream.

It was great. Even with just being a boy, I realized how lucky we were. Everything that was on the table with the exception of the salt, butter and cream, the milk we kids drank and the coffee that my parents drank had come from the garden or from the lake where I fished.

It was a home grown fish fry. There are few people today that would have a meal any better than that or could even put a meal like that on the table anymore. Gardens are disappearing, canning is a lost art, and family dinner time is fading away as well.

But I can remember when almost everyone had a garden and the entire family sat down every night to eat dinner after one of the kids gave thanks. I can remember fresh fish made simply and fresh vegetables and fruit from the garden and what a wondrous taste that they had. I think I was very lucky.

A SOFT DAY

I first heard the expression when I was in Ireland. Our bus driver and tour guide looked outside one morning as we were eating breakfast and said "we are having a soft day today."

Then he added, "It is a bit moist outside."

I looked out. It was not just raining. It was pouring. Water was running down the windows and washing the ancient streets of this old Irish town. Apparently they have a lot of this kind of weather in Ireland and they seem to take it in stride.

I woke sometime in the early morning when it still was dark. I could hear the rumble of thunder. Later about mid morning when I finally did get up I was met with dark gray skies that promised rain. The Bass Queen turned on the weather station as I made coffee. After watching a few minutes and before the coffee was done she announced that it looked like it was going to be raining any minute.

By the time I had got the morning newspapers and was sipping my first cup of coffee, the rain began. It started as a few sprinkles. By the time I had finished the first newspaper and first cup of coffee the rain was splashing down on our back deck and running down the windows.

"A soft day today," I said to myself. "It is a bit moist outside."

The Bass Queen and I had planned to go fishing but she cancelled out as the first light sprinkles came down. I did not have the energy to find anyone else and lost any motivation to go by myself as the rain began to beat against the house. So I finished the other newspaper and poured another cup of coffee and wandered downstairs to the Supply Room.

The Supply Room is the basement. In addition to the artificial Christmas tree and the boxes of holiday decorations, with packing boxes and bags of wrapping paper that sits against one wall, it is the repository of my hunting and fishing gear. In the middle of the room sits nine rod racks normally filled with rods. Since it is the fishing season fifteen or twenty rods have been moved to the garage or are in the rod locker of the boat. In a corner I have a dresser where I store some of the clothing such as hats, gloves, long underwear and that type of thing. On top of it, is an electrical line winder that I use to spool lines on reels. Next to it is the gun safe. I have two work benches that have reels, tools and various baits and fishing equipment stacked on them.

Another wall has a metal bar where hunting and fishing clothing hangs and there are four old Army foot lockers stocked on the top of each other, filled with various packs, bags, more reels and assorted equipment. There are a number of tackle boxes scattered about. There is another pile of about half a dozen ice chests and then shelves which store sleeping bags, tents, rucksacks, stoves, lanterns, boxes of baits, pots and pans and more camping and fishing gear. Under the stairway are a dozen mallard decoys, a dozen and a half diver duck decoys and three floater Canada goose decoys.

It is my Supply Room. After spending twenty two years in the Army I know a supply room when I see it. On damp days it even smells like an Army supply room and today it brings back memories to me. A lot of adventures start from supply rooms and my Supply Room is no different.

Against one table is a stack of spinning rods that need to be restrung. There are two large plastic boxes that still have not been completely unloaded from fishing trips to Canada two months earlier and North Dakota just a couple of weeks ago. There is a pile of clothes sitting on top of those boxes that have been washed but not put away after those trips.

This "soft day" and cancelled fishing now gives me the time to take care of these chores. With the electric line winder I pull off the line from the reels and restring them. One of the reels gets twelve pound, several get ten pound and two others get eight pound. I put leaders on several of the lines and place them in rod racks. One rod needs a new tip so I rummage around on the work bench until I find one that will fit and glue it on.

The clothing gets hung up finally and then I open up the plastic boxes. I wonder back upstairs to put away extra food stuff in the kitchen and to fill my coffee cup and return to the Supply Room. Fillet knives, pans and cooking utensils are placed on the shelves.

There is no sense of urgency here. I am taking my time. There are lots of trips back to the kitchen for more coffee and there is some general picking up to do in the Supply Room and I even take a break to call a fishing buddy and arrange a fishing trip mid week with him. I remember that there is a rod in the garage that I need to work on so I fix the rod and replace a bait on another rod that is in the boat.

This soft day slips away. It is now late afternoon. My chores are done and I have a lazy feeling of contentment. The Bass Queen dispatches me off to the grocery store for some things she needs for dinner. It is still moist outside but it has been a good day.

REDISCOVERING PANFISH

Like most fishermen, the first fish that I remember catching was a bluegill. Most of my initial childhood fishing memories revolve around bluegills or many of its other panfish cousins such as sunfish, pumpkinseeds, crappies and others.

When I lived in Alabama some almost thirty years ago, I still was catching a lot of bluegill or as they call them in the Deep South brim or bream. I still can remember going to the bait shop early in the morning to get crickets for a day of brim fishing and listening to the almost deafening chirping of the crickets in that small, closed bait shot.

Then I bought a boat and I became too sophisticated for panfish. I became a bass fisherman.

Occasionally, I would still pull my boat into some flooded timber on one of my favorite lakes down there and drop minnows next to the trees and catch a few crappies. And there was a little pond on a horse farm that I fished. Every spring one of my buddies and I would switch one afternoon from chasing bass on that pond to using our fly rods with poppers to catch a mess of brim.

However, from the time I bought that boat I was caught with the bass bug and it did not take long before I had abandoned panfish. In the years after, I ended up catching a bunch of bass in Alabama, North Carolina and Virginia and then after a four year stint in Germany I returned to the Midwest. First in Minneapolis and then, after retiring from the Army, buying a home in Hudson, Wisconsin. I was catching lots of bass in the Midwest and seldom would ever consider trifling my time away on panfish.

Ever so slowly that began to change. I had bought a new bass boat and had thrown in a couple of fly rods in the bottom of the rod locker. Maybe someday we will try fly fishing for some bluegills I told my wife, the Bass Queen. But we really did not seriously consider panfish in our pursuit of the bass.

One late spring day we were bass fishing one of our favorite bass lakes near our home in Hudson and we found a large school of bluegills in a small, shallow bay. The bass were not very cooperative this particular day and it was the Bass Queen who suggested that we might finally get out those fly rods.

So we did and in the next couple of hours we caught a bunch of bluegills and put about a dozen and a half of the larger ones in the livewell. It was fun fishing. In fact it was a lot of fun fishing. When we got home I filleted the fish and put them in the freezer. Several months later when the snow was falling around our house and the wind was drifting the snow across my driveway, I took those fillets out of the freezer, thawed them and deep fried them for dinner. They tasted great. My singular pursuit of bass began to crack a little.

The final blow that broke it was a day several years later with my buddy, Scott. It was early summer and again it was a day that the bass weren't hitting very well on a lake in northern Wisconsin. Out of frustration, Scott pulled out an ultralight spinning rod and started casting a small tube jig. He caught three or four crappies and I hadn't had a strike on my bass gear when I finally broke down. The winter before I had bought one of those ultralight noodle rods just in case I might want to try it on panfish; now was the time.

In the next couple of hours, Scott and I caught a couple dozen crappies. On that noodle rod they put up a great fight and, once again, I was rediscovering what great fun it was to catch panfish. It was a couple of days later that I fried those fish and again recognized what great tasting fish they were.

From then on, I began to devote more time to fishing for panfish and I finally realized what fun panfish can be. They are easy to fish for and, as I take a lot of younger fishermen in my boat that is important for them. For me I have found what a good fight panfish put up on ultralight spinning gear. As well for me and the number of guests, that visit our house every summer, we take great delight in what a fine tasting fish they are. It is hard to find a better meal than fresh panfish fillets on a hot summer night when they were caught earlier in the day and are now deep fried and eaten with coleslaw and potato salad or French fries with an ice cold beer.

I now spend a lot more time fishing for panfish and I am glad for that. It truly is fun. Just the other day, The Bass Queen and I interrupted our bass fishing for a couple of hours and caught a bunch of bluegills on small tube jigs. We didn't keep any of the fish but we fished them just for the fun of it. A couple of days later my friend, Dennis and I took his nephews, thirteen year old Andre and six year old Mike, fishing for bluegills. We caught over sixty fish and they took home twenty six of the bigger ones for dinner.

It was pure joy to watch those boys catch those fish and in their faces and their smiles I saw another younger fisherman half a century ago that thought that the bluegill was the finest fish in the whole world. Although I had turned my back on panfish for a lot of years, I have rediscovered them now and I will never again ignore them.

INDIAN CEMETERY

We were motoring up a Canadian river in search of rapids where we expected to find walleyes for our evening fish fry. It was a cool day that kept us in rain gear. Light gray clouds swirled overhead and an occasional hole would allow a patch of blue to poke through. It had rained every day since we had flown into our outpost cabin and it looked like we would get wet again before we would get back to our cabin in the early evening.

Tall, thin, dark green pine trees on shore swayed gently in the wind. This blue ribbon of water ran through this rugged land. Large boulders climbed up the hills alongside the river. A few swampy bays opened up on the sides of the river. As we motored upstream we saw an eagle and got a fleeting glimpse of a moose as it silently disappeared into the woods from the waters edge. Brown piles of sticks could be seen along the banks where beavers made their houses.

I had been told about this by our outfitter and I was looking for it. There was an Indian cemetery on the high ground above this stretch of the river. I had been up and down this river two or three times earlier and had not seen it. This time I was looking for it.

We rounded a bend in the river and there it was. On a small hill, right next to the river was the cemetery. How I had missed it the other times I do not know.

Around it towered spruce trees but the cemetery itself looked clear. There were, as I counted them from the river, six wooden crosses rising from the floor of the forest. There might have been more further back where I could not see. There was grass on the cemetery and amazingly enough it was short as if someone had cut it.

I asked my fishing partner to turn off the motor and we gently drifted in the current below the cemetery. There was no sound. It was if nature recognized it as hallowed ground.

I had no interest in getting out of the boat and exploring the cemetery. I would have been disrespectful to those who were there and their people who put them there. I have never considered cemeteries to be tourist spots and if I had gone up there it would be as if I was a tourist.

The summer before I had visited Omaha Beach and to get to the beach you had to walk through the cemetery there. The neat rows of white crosses against the bright green grass and brilliant blue skies were humbling and emotional. A tear came to my eye as I saw a grave marker inscribed with, "Here rests in honored glory a comrade in arms known but to God." Hallowed ground.

Later this fall I will visit Arlington when I am in Washington D.C. I will be in the capital as a tourist but will go to Arlington to pay my respect to Tombs of the Unknown Soldiers and at the grave of President Kennedy. More hallowed ground.

As I looked at the Indian cemetery from our boat on the water, I wondered how those people had gotten there.

Was there an Indian village nearby once? If not, why were those bodies brought there to be buried?

There is nothing near here. No roads. Just the river. We had taken a twenty minute float plane ride from Pickle Lake, Ontario to get to the lake that this river empties into. And Pickle Lake is as far north that one can drive on pavement in Ontario. This Indian cemetery is certainly isolated.

Does anyone come here to morn these peoples' passing or gather here on special occasions to remember their dead family members or friends? Are their names on the graves? I suppose that I could have answered that question on my own if I have pulled up on shore to personally look at the cemetery. Or were they known but to God?

I felt a sense of sadness come over me as I looked at the Indian cemetery from our boat while it drifted with the current and the wind. I told my fishing partner to start the motor and take us further upriver.

But then perhaps there is no need for sadness. This cemetery is in a beautiful spot and those people are resting where they wanted to be in the land that they had lived on and conquered during their time on earth. More hallowed ground.

HEY BOY . . .

In the course of the twenty plus years that I served in the United States Army, I spent almost half that time in the deep south in places like Missouri, North Carolina and a couple of times in Alabama. Although I was a yankee from the north woods of Wisconsin, I adapted fairly well to living in the land of Dixie.

I spent the most amount of time in Alabama. I was in the central part of Alabama between Birmingham, Alabama and Atlanta, Georgia. They had hardwoods forests there that reminded me of northern Wisconsin and at least once every winter we even got a light dusting of snow. In Alabama the world came to a standstill with even the least bit of snow. We yankees would laugh and just continue on, telling our shocked southern friends that there really is no need for concern until you get over a foot of white stuff.

It was in Alabama that I learned to bass fish and I will be eternally grateful for that. All my northern fishing experiences had revolved around trout and walleyes. If you ever want to see an incredulous look on a southerners face just tell them about ice fishing. They won't believe you but then again they all think that us yankees are nuts anyway.

There were lots of things about the south that I loved. I loved that I could fish out of a boat all year long. I loved

131

the laid back, slower pace of life I found in the south and I loved southern cooking.

Southern fried chicken, country fired steak, corn bread, hush puppies, sausage gravy and biscuits are just a few of the incredible foods I found while living in the south. But there were a couple of southern specialties that I never was able to develop a taste for. One of them was grits. They suggested putting sugar on them, jelly, butter, syrup, mixing them with your eggs. The only thing I did not do was pour bourbon on them. That would have been a waste of good booze. I never found a way to eat grits that I liked.

The other southern food that I never got to like was catfish. Down south, catfish have been elevated to legendary status. Some of my southern friends have waxed so elegantly about catfish that you would think that they were talking about lobster. The south is littered with catfish houses and they all claim to make the world's best catfish.

I've tried my best over the years to find a way to eat catfish. But having spent most of my Yankee life eating walleyes, perch and trout; catfish was a tough sell. I do know that even in the north we have catfish and I had caught several of them in my earlier days. I used to pick up a few channel cats every spring while fishing for walleyes and white bass on the Wolf River and once in my teen years I caught a five pound blue cat in the channels near my home.

I always admitted that catfish put up a great fight but I never found them to be worthwhile putting on the table. I tried a lot of different recipes and techniques. Once when I lived in Missouri, I caught a bunch of bluegills and a fairly good sized catfish. I brought them home and had a big fish fry. One of my southern buddies raved about how good my catfish was. I tried it. It was horrible. He had spent over ten years in the Army at this point and it made me wonder if all those pots of Army coffee had altered his taste buds.

One early Sunday morning I was fishing on the raceway just below a dam in Alabama. I found lots of bluegill there. They call them bream down south. I set myself up on the bank with a lawn chair, a small bucket of red worms and two light spinning rods propped up on rocks. I was steadily catching bluegills and was filling up a live basket with them. But every now and then my line would shoot out and when I set the hook I could feel that it was bigger fish then those bluegills I was catching. It would be a catfish.

Although they had been fun to catch I had no interest in keeping them so I twisted the hook out of them and threw the fish back in the water. There was a father and son sitting about fifty yards below me and they looked shocked as they saw me release that catfish. After the second time that I did that, the father felt compelled to come over and speak to me.

"Hey boy, now listen here," he said to me. "If you don't be wanting them there catfish don't be throwing them back in the water. You give me a shout and I'll send my boy over to get them from you. Them are good fish."

So a few minutes later I caught another catfish and I gave him a shout and a young boy came over to get it, leaving me with a "thank you, sir" as he ran back with the fish. In the course of the next couple of hours I caught another four or five catfish. They weren't particularly big. They were all about two or three pounds or as they would say just the right eating size. But that father and son seemed happy with them.

Now as I have been writing this I have developed a hunger for some country fried steak and eggs. I think I will have to go out and get a plate of that. Also I am starting to feel guilty about those catfish. Perhaps I have been a bit too harsh. I will be back down south this fall and I think I will find myself a catfish house and give it a try again. I will have to have hush puppies, too.

FISHING ON TUESDAY

One of the nice things about writers is that we really do not have a "real" job. Yes we do work and there are times that writing can be difficult. Sometimes it gets frustrating when the words do not seem to be coming along. In the old days it was a blank piece of paper in a typewriter but today we stare at a blank computer screen.

We do not have normal hours like most working folks. We can write whenever we want or can find the time. Some writers write in the morning, others at night. I generally write during the day but it seems that I end up in my office all hours of the day or night jotting down notes or ideas. That is part of the work of being a writer.

I carry notebooks with me all the time now. I have several note books plus several more pads of paper with more notes and ideas floating around my office. I have notebooks in my van and even in my boat. I have been known to stop fishing and pull out a notebook and write out some notes for a future story.

Writers are always working, although they may not be conforming to a normal work routine. By the same token we have the luxury to do other things while most other people are working normal jobs with normal hours. You must also understand that normal people, with normal jobs, and normal hours generally get paid better than we writers with our strange schedules. There are always trade offs in life.

So it happened that I went fishing on a Tuesday. A couple of days earlier I had called my buddy Ben. He works retail in a sports store. He works some rather odd hours himself. He was off on Tuesday. I had been wanting to get out on the Mississippi River and try some new baits. We writers call that research.

It was an early spring morning. Gray clouds hung close to the horizon and there was a hint of rain in the air. Everything seemed hazy and subdued. A brisk wind with a chill to it blew down the river.

We noticed that there were just a few cars in the parking lot. Normally on the weekend the parking lot would be packed and the overflow would be parking along the road. Perhaps only other writers and retail workers with a day off were fishing today.

We blasted down the river, pulling up at the dam. There were only two or three boats there. Fishing on Tuesday had significantly reduced the normal crowd. With our research baits tied to our lines I moved the boat close to the bank and we started flipping our lures against the rocky shore. On about my fourth or fifth cast my bait stopped and I could feel a fish pulling away with it. I set the hook and my light spinning rod began to bounce as the fish dove for the bottom. I turned the fish but it stubbornly stayed deep. Slowly I began to get the fish closer to the boat and a moment or two later it was splashing on the surface. Grabbing the line I hauled the fish into the boat. It was a two pound white bass. We took a quick photo and I slipped the fish back into the water.

A couple of minutes later, Ben had a fish. It also was a white bass. We continued to work the bank and were steadily catching white bass. No matter what you might think about white bass, they do put up a great fight. Several times we both had fish on at the same time.

Once Ben snagged a large carp and pandemonium reigned as the fish surged off with little chance of stopping. The fish rolled on the surface, impervious to the pressure of Ben's light rod and line. It took quite a while before Ben could get the fish close enough so that we could pull the hooks out of its tail with a pliers. We estimated that the fish went about twenty five pounds.

A little later I set the hook and the fish would not budge. It put up a tenacious bull dog fight that was more than any white bass. It turned out to be a seven or eight pound dog fish. I had never caught one before. White bass may never win any prizes for beauty but this dog fish was down right ugly. Ben also caught a gar fish and I got a small sturgeon. What an assortment of fish.

The white bass continued to hit all day long and by late afternoon we guessed that we probably caught and released over seventy five of them. It had been a great day of fishing. It was a great Tuesday.

Ben and I both realized that we were lucky to be there. We could be working but we weren't. We had jobs that let us go fishing on a Tuesday. My research baits worked. They helped to justify going fishing. I wasn't just fishing. I was doing research so I really was working.

I reached into my waterproof box and pulled out my notebook. As the wind and current drifted us down the river I quickly jotted down notes. There is a story or two here. I had not been just goofing off all day in the middle of the week. I actually had a job to do.

ANOTHER RULING

We had been muskie fishing on a small lake south of the Twin Cities. It had been a beautiful day. For a late summer day it had not been too hot and a slight wind kept us cool while barely ruffling the surface of the water. It had been hazy and the sun kept trying to break through the light gray cloud cover but had not succeeded.

Doug and I had thrown a variety of baits but we had not turned a fish. That is the nature of muskie fishing. If you have spent a day muskie fishing and just get a follow then musky fishermen get all excited. In our case we never even had that, so there had not been much excitement.

Sometimes I wonder why I muskie fish. I have, over the years, spent a lot of money on musky fishing rods and reels and baits. In case you had not noticed, muskie baits aren't cheap. I have spent a lot of time on the water throwing very large, expensive baits with very little reward.

For all the days that I have spent muskie fishing I can count on one hand the number of muskies I have caught while actually muskie fishing. I have caught three times that many muskies by accident while bass fishing.

So why do we do it? The answer is simple. We musky fish because no matter how long it takes, when you do catch one it is one heck of a thrill. I remember one of the muskies

I actually caught while muskie fishing. I caught it on a figure eight right next to the boat. When I set the hook the water just exploded as if someone had set off a bomb right next to the boat.

There are few things as satisfying in the outdoors as catching a big muskie. Sometimes it is just exciting to see them.

Another time I was fishing near Boulder Junction in northeastern Wisconsin. My nephew Scott, who was probably about thirteen at the time, was in the boat with me. I heard a big splash at the back of the boat and I quickly turned to look to make sure that Scott had not fallen off the back of the boat. Scott had not fallen overboard but had a wild eyed look on his face. "It looked like a shark," he said. Since it was a little far north for sharks I figured he had seen a big muskie.

Even if most of your muskies are small, there is always the possibility that the next cast will give you that fifty inch trophy. You can go from a lousy day of muskie fishing to a great day of muskie fishing with one cast.

So with that, Dough and I continue to muskie fish. There will be that day and that cast with the right bait that will give us that trophy we have dreamed of. Dreams are good. They keep you going.

But this day was not going to be it. It was early evening and we finally gave up. We will be back another day. We loaded the boat on the trailer and headed north, back to the Twin Cities.

As we were driving home it came to me that Doug and I were skunked. We didn't even get a follow up or a swirl. We were flat out skunked. But again, that is the nature of muskie fishing.

Now Doug and I take getting skunked seriously. We don't like it. It ranks right up there with hemorrhoids and root canals on the fun scale. For most of the fishing season we do not get skunked except for muskie fishing.

Then it dawned on me. If getting skunked is the norm for muskie fishing; then if you spend a day muskie fishing and get skunked does it really count as being skunked?

I posed the question to Doug. "What do you think," I asked. I consider Doug to be The Commissioner. He has been instrumental in making these determinations on other occasions. We have, in the past, made various intricate decisions on when to count a fish or not or on the validity of being skunked in different situations. But the muskie issue has not been brought up until now.

I was driving so I could not watch Doug. I heard nothing from him for some time and wondered if he had fallen asleep. I took my eyes off the road for just a second to check on him. Doug was deep in thought. This is serious stuff. There are consequences to this decision. This could have a reaching affect.

Finally Doug spoke. He talked about the basic tenets of muskie fishing and how you spend far more time on the water trying to catch a muskie and there is a small percentage of that time that you truly do catch a muskie. And muskie fishermen continue to go fishing fully aware of this. They need a break he felt.

"So therefore, if you are muskie fishing, knowing full well that your chances of not catching a muskie is far greater than actually catching one. And if you have spent the entire fishing trip muskie fishing and had not taken a fish then I don't think it should count as a skunk," he opined.

"Now understand," he continued. "If you had become bored with muskie fishing and took a break to, let say, go bass fishing and still did not catch a fish then that counts as a skunk. But if you have been musky fishing the whole time it doesn't count."

I concurred completely. I breathed a sigh of relief. His ruling just wiped out a bunch of skunks out of the record book for me.

I HAVE THE POWER

I do not know where I got this from but I have the power to change the weather. This generally happens to me in the early spring or the late fall when I am fishing on the Mississippi River.

Regardless of how nice the weather may be; all that I have to do is start getting ready to go fishing. Then the weather will immediately turn bad. This is not a once or twice kind of thing with me. It happens regularly enough to me that I really do believe that I have this power.

On one recent mid November Sunday afternoon my buddy Doug and I were driving back from a hunting trip and we started talking about going fishing on the river. It was a sunny day with clear blue skies and the temperatures were in the low 60s.

We made some tentative plans to get on the river the following weekend. A couple of days later I called him at home and we set up the times for leaving and coordinated the other considerations, such as lunch and bait, that have to be made in planning a trip. It was still warm outside.

The very next day about noon when The Bass Queen came home from work I looked outside and there was a slight snow flurry going on.

"Is that snow?" I asked.

"Well, ya," she said giving me this look that said "you have lived all these years in the Midwest and you can't recognize snow."

"Well it figures," I said. "I'm going fishing this weekend."

"I wished you had told me a little earlier so I could have gotten the car washed before the weather went bad."

Even the Bass Queen believes that I have the power to change the weather.

A few minutes later we left to meet friends for lunch. Two hours later when we left a little bar and grill in town the snow was coming down much heavier and a cold cutting wind was howling off the river a block away.

"Good work," The Bass Queen said. "If you had stayed home this weekend it probably could have been nice enough for sun bathing."

This happens to me all the time in the fall and the spring. It doesn't matter how nice the weather is, as soon as I start getting the boat ready or call one of my buddies to start planning a fishing trip the weather will radically change; always for the worst.

One early spring the temperatures soared. People were walking around wearing shorts. You would have thought it was summer. A warm sun beat down and skies were cloudless. You people have no idea what is next I thought to myself, but I do.

I gave a call to one of my buddies.

"You want to go fishing on Saturday," I asked him.

"Sure," he said. "It will be great to get outside in this nice spring weather."

I did not have the heart to tell him. He had no idea what he was getting into.

Friday night, he and his wife stayed with us as we were leaving early the next morning. Outside a frigid mix of rain and snow was pounding against the window on our deck.

"Nice going," The Bass Queen said to me when I went into the kitchen to mix a drink. "You have messed up the weekend for everybody."

"I didn't mean too," I said. "I just planned on going fishing."

"I suppose you didn't tell him either."

"No I didn't." I said. "I thought he might back out."

"Poor guy. I sure hope that he brought his long johns and winter jacket."

THE PITH HELMET

The Bass Queen and I are eating breakfast at our favorite breakfast spot in Key West, Florida. The place is called the Blue Heaven. It has had a colorful past. Where once had been a bordello is now a gift shop. The grounds at one time used to have a boxing ring and Ernest Hemingway, who only lived a few blocks away in the 1930s, used to referee matches there. But now the boxing ring is gone and where it probably stood has outdoor tables for people like The Bass Queen and I.

The Blue Heaven makes wonderful breakfasts and on this warm, sunny December day, The Bass Queen and I are eating what I think is their signature dish, lobster benedict. I looked over at the table next to us and I see another couple also eating breakfast. They seem normal in every way but the man is wearing a pith helmet.

Although you can see practically anything in Key West, you do not normally see a lot of pith helmets and it looked particularly unusual. This couple finished their breakfast before we did and left while I was finishing my last cup of coffee.

"Did you see that couple at the table next to us?" I asked The Bass Queen.

"The guy in the pith helmet?"

145

"Ya him." I said. "When we were kids remember when in the westerns the good guys always wore white hats and the bad guys all wore black hats?" The Bass Queen nodded. It seemed in those days cowboys only wore white or black hats. But then again we only had black and white television.

"In the jungle movies," I continued. "The good guys all wore fancy bush hats and the bad guys always wore pith helmets."

When I was a kid one of my favorite actors was a British actor named Stewart Granger. He was in a lot of jungle movies with safaris and shooting lions and elephants and searching for lost treasures in the jungle. He was always the good Bwana and wore a stylish bush hat. The bad bwanas that were evil and treacherous all had pith helmets.

Probably the pith helmet got a lot of bad press in those days because of the bad bwana stereotyping. But actually the pith has a storied past. It was issued to the British Army in the tropics for years. I believe that our own post office mail delivery people have pith helmets for summer wear. At one time in our own Army, the first drill sergeants wore pith helmets but shortly thereafter they switched to the campaign hat, also known as the smoky the bear hat, that those of us who have gone through basic training remember so well. Perhaps the drill sergeants did not want to project the bad bwana image.

The Bass Queen and I spent the next several hours walking around and shopping on Duval Street in Key West and we ended up running into the guy with the pith helmet a couple of more times. Probably I would have never recognized the guy again but it was hard to be inconspicuous in a pith helmet.

Later in the afternoon we had wandered down to the ocean front where I stopped in at a fishing store that I always visit. The Bass Queen went in with me but after about twenty minutes she said that she was going to take a look at some of the other shops. I finished browsing and walked out to find The Bass Queen. I found her in a hat shop and as I walked into the store she turned to see me and yelled "look what I found." She was holding a pith helmet.

"Try it on," she said. The pith helmet was very light, shaded the neck as well as the face and sat on the head leaving a cushion of air that would make it cooler to wear on hot sunny days. "You look good in it," she said. "You want it." I couldn't make up my mind. It would make a good summer fishing hat. But it cost about forty dollars. Although I will spend that amount on a lot sillier stuff and will probably loose more than that in crankbaits during the fishing season, it did seem a lot for a hat considering that most baseball caps cost less then ten dollars.

I said that I would think about it. We never got back to the hat shop in the remaining days before we left for home and I had forgotten about the pith helmet. Two weeks later The Bass Queen and I were exchanging our Christmas presents. She had already surprised me with a couple of things when she handed me a large box. When I opened it I found the pith helmet. On the afternoon that we left Key West she called back down to the hat shop, ordered it and had them ship it to her.

I must admit now that I have it, I will wear it this summer while fishing. So if you are fishing in western Wisconsin and see a guy wearing a pith helmet that might be me. I just got to get over the bad bwana thing.

THE IMPROMPTU FISHING TRIP

I had just walked in the door when the phone rang. I dropped the stuff that was in my hand and grabbed the phone. It was my fishing buddy Doug.

"What are you doing this afternoon?" He asked.

I always have stories to write and there were a couple that I needed to work on.

"What do you have in mind?" I asked.

"Do you want to go fishing?" He replied.

I thought about it for an instant. Yes I have stories to write but then it is summer. I can go fishing now. I can always write during the winter. It really wasn't a hard decision.

"Sure," I said. "Where do you want to go?"

Within another minute it was all worked out. We were going to Deer Lake which is north of where I live. Doug would pick me up in about an hour. He would be bringing a friend of his along as well.

"Don't forget to bring rain gear," Doug said as he was hanging up. "It is supposed to rain a bit."

Doug's friend was a young man named John and in the hour or so drive it took us to get to the lake John quickly became another fishing buddy. It doesn't take long to become buddies when you have fishing in common.

By the time we got to Deer Lake gray, angry clouds swirled overhead and as we pulled away in the boat from the dock at the landing. It began to sprinkle. We quickly put on rain gear. It was short ride down the lake and when Doug finally pulled back on the throttle of the motor and the boat slid to a stop we were on the opposite side of the lake.

On my fourth cast a fish hit the bait and I pulled back to set the hook. It felt like a good sized fish as it tore off, pulling line from my light spinning rod. The fish put up a head strong fight. I thought at first that it was a big bass but as I got the fish closer I could see that it was long and thin. It was a muskie. It wasn't particularly big by muskie standards but it went about twenty or so inches. It always is neat to catch a muskie no matter what size they are.

"Catching a muskie is always a great way to start a fishing trip," Doug said as he took my photo before I slipped the fish back into the water. A few casts later I caught a foot long bass. Then Doug caught a fish and finally John scored on a bass.

The rain continued to drip down. It would stop for a few minutes and then start again. It never stopped long enough for us to seriously consider getting out of rain gear. Even when it did stop for a few minutes the gray, ugly skies told us that more rain was not far away. It was one of those rains that did not ever really soak into anything. It just seemed to make everything damp.

All afternoon long, with the rain dripping off the bills of our hats, we continued to catch fish. There were times that two of us would have fish on at the same time and once all three of us had a fish on. I was glad that I was fishing instead of working. I can always write that story tomorrow but you never know when you can go fishing next so you need to take advantage of every opportunity even if it is totally unplanned.

The fish were in the weeds and we were using shallow running crankbaits that ran right over the top of them. The fish came tearing out the weeds to attack our baits. The water was clear enough that at times you could see a flash of silver in the water before you could feel the fish hit the bait. It is always fun to see a fish hit your lure.

Later in the afternoon we used plastic worms around docks and the fish continued to hit them. I switched to a couple of other shallow running baits that worked well around weeds and they caught fish as well.

Regardless of how gloomy the weather was we steadily caught fish all afternoon and by the time we quit in the early evening we had caught and released over fifty bass plus my little muskie. None of the bass were particularly large but they were fun to catch and they had all put up a good fight.

It had been a good day of fishing and I was glad that I had not succumbed to work and had fallen to the temptation to go fishing instead. Last minute invitations can at times open a new world to you that you had not planned on. There is nothing wrong with planning but it can take the spontaneity out of things. With the hectic pressures and schedules of our modern life we can all probably use a few more impromptu fishing trips.

IMMORTALITY

A hundred and four years ago tomorrow my grandfather was born. He was born in Russia in a small town that probably no longer exists, on the banks of the Volga River. As a boy he immigrated with his family to America and eventually settled in Sheboygan, Wisconsin.

It was here in this small town on Lake Michigan that he grew into manhood and married my grandmother. In 1924 my mother, their only child, was born. With the exception of a few trips, he would spend the rest of his life in Wisconsin.

I was his oldest grandchild and for a number of years his only grandson. He was the person who taught me how to fish and still to this day I remember what great adventures it was to go fishing with Grandpa. We were fishing buddies.

We most often fished the Fox River in Oshkosh in the spring for the walleye and white bass run. In the summer we fished Lake Winnebago which was less than a mile from my parent's house.

He had a small wooden boat that was covered in fiberglass and a green Kiekhaefer Mercury three and a half horse motor. By today's standards it isn't much of a boat but in the days of my youth it was a grand fishing boat.

Grandpa would let me drive that boat. It might have only been a three and a half horse motor but it sure seemed awesome to me. We would motor out into Lake Winnebago. Suddenly he would yell stop, I would turn off the motor and he would drop the anchor.

We would then start catching fish. It seemed that simple in those days. Now mind you Lake Winnebago is no little lake. It is seven miles wide and over twenty miles long. How he would know when to stop is beyond me to this day but we always caught fish.

Grandpa knew what he was doing. I have old black and white photographs of he and I holding stringers of walleyes and white bass to prove it. I remember seeing recently an advertisement that went something like, "do you remember when your fish finder and GPS was wrapped in an efficient unit called Grandpa." That was my grandpa.

Unfortunately, my grandfather died young. He was only sixty seven when he died from a heart attack while shoveling snow in a blizzard on the second to last day of 1971. I was stunned that morning when my father called to tell me. I was twenty two at the time and thought Grandpa would live forever and would someday teach my son how to fish as he had taught me.

It has now been thirty seven years since Grandpa has passed away. He left me with a tackle box full of memories and stories that I have shared. I am amazed after all these years, all the people that have I met and all the adventures and travels I have had, since he has been gone, how often I think of him and how often I tell stories about him.

One of my favorite is when he first was teaching me how to fish. We were allowed to use two rods in those days. Grandpa hated to lose fish. He seemed to take it personally. So, if I missed too many strikes he thought it was because I was not concentrating enough. He would take one of the rods away from me so it would be easier for me to concentrate with just one rod. I was not happy with that. I wanted to fish with two rods just like the big guys did. So I worked hard not to miss too many strikes or to lose fish once I set the hook. Grandpa taught me well. To this day I do not lose many fish.

I have told that story and others about Grandpa to my wife, all my fishing buddies, my daughters and son, my sons-in-law and anyone else that is in my boat. I have a captive audience in the boat so they get exposed to all the stories. It is amazing that even today when I do miss a few fish inevitably the other person in the boat will say to me "your grandpa would take a rod away from you."

My grandpa has lived on for a couple of more generations through the stories that I have written and told about him. And perhaps he will live for a few more generations longer as my children and eventually my grandchild will repeat the stories about him. I think that is immortality or at least as close as anyone is ever going to get to it.

That is the only way that any of us will become immortal. It is through the memories that others will have of us long after we are gone that will allow us to live on in this world. I would like to think that I will live on through the stories that my children and grandchildren will tell about me after I am no longer here.

This last week my six year old grandson was fishing with me for a few days. So the process starts again.

One evening before I read him a book just before he went to bed, I asked him if he knew who taught me how to fish. He said, "Your grandpa." So one day he might ask his grandson that same question and get the same answer. Then I might live on. I might achieve some sense of immortality too.

VOODOO TRAILER

I believe that my boat trailer is possessed by a spirit. The strangest things happen to my boat trailer that I, nor anyone else, can truly explain. It must be voodoo.

At the beginning of this fishing season, when I took my boat into the Boat Doctor for its spring checkup, I asked that they replace the left back light on the trailer. It had been having problems all last year and had completely died by the end of the season. When I picked the boat up the left backlight worked perfectly. But not for long.

Within a couple of weeks it wasn't working. I changed the bulb and it worked. Two weeks later I noticed that the light was out again. I can not tell you how many bulbs I have been through and it is only a couple of months into the fishing season. I now carry several packages of light bulbs in my van.

A week ago I noticed that the light was out again. We were sitting at a landing and while my fishing buddy was rigging up a couple of rods before we launched the boat I thought it was the ideal time to change the bulb. It worked fine. Less than a week later as another fishing buddy was backing up the van and trailer so that I could push off the boat, I noticed that the light was not working again.

As I recall I swore some very nasty things about that particular light. That evening when I got home I mentioned it to my wife, The Bass Queen, that I needed to change that light again. She told me that I didn't need to. I asked why. She told me that all the lights were working fine when she saw me back the trailer down the driveway when I got home. How can that light not work and then a couple of hours later be working. I think that it is voodoo.

Once last season I was leaving the Mississippi River where I had been trolling for walleyes. As I was driving through Prescott I saw a police car with its lights on in my rear view window. I pulled over. A nice young policewoman came up to the window to tell me that my trailer lights weren't working. They had been working when I left home. She took my license and went back to her police car and I got out and pulled the plug out of the trailer and then joined the plug back together. The lights worked.

"They seem to be working now," the police lady said as she handed back my license. Half an hour later when I got home the lights were not working again. It is voodoo.

But it just isn't the lights. I was driving through a small central Wisconsin town one afternoon returning home from a mid October fishing trip. I looked in the rear window to see one of my trailer wheels wobbling. I pulled over and got out to find that the left axel was split and spewing out grease. I limped the trailer two blocks to a gas station. I went inside and talked to a young lady, explaining my predicament. She told me that her husband knew how to fix it. She made a telephone call and then told me that her husband would be right down after the Packer game was over. Being a Packer fan myself I fully understood his need to finish the game.

He showed up after the game, sent me off to a store for parts and then fixed it. I was delayed by a couple of hours but the axel was like new. Now being like new on my trailer does not mean anything. I keep checking the axel regularly and keep putting in grease. A couple of years later I noticed that there was grease on the inside of the tire. It was the left axel again. I called The Boat Doctor and they told me to bring it in right away. They replaced a bunch of parts, put in more grease and told me that it was fine. I asked Scott, who always works on my boat at The Boat Doctor, as to how can this happen twice to a trailer that was less than fives years old. He told me that he had no idea as to how it could happen twice since he had never seen it happen once to any other trailer.

Last summer it happened again. You guessed it; it was the left side of the axel again. The axel blew out just as I was backing the boat back down the driveway after coming home from a fishing trip. I had to call a tow truck to get it and take it to a mechanic. The Boat Doctor ordered parts and it is now fixed again. I am wondering what else can go wrong and when.

I have noticed a pattern here, however. It is always the left side. It is the left light or the left axel. I think this is strange. It has to be voodoo.

THE TWO HUNDRED DOLLAR
BOAT RIDE

By the time that March finally comes around most of us are sick and tired of winter. By the end of March I will be getting out on the Mississippi River for walleyes and sauger but before that happens there will be a couple of snowstorms and more ice and nasty weather to contend with. So usually I try to go to someplace warm for a week or so in the first half of March.

This year my wife, the Bass Queen, and I went to Cabo San Lucas on the tip of the Baja Peninsula in Mexico. Although any place warm that time of the year sounds appealing it was even more attractive by its reputation for great fishing.

One early morning when it was still dark and the temperatures were hovering about zero, the Bass Queen and I boarded a plane. Four hours later we landed where it was hot and sunny. This was what we had come for.

Within a couple of hours I was sitting in a chair next to the pool with a gin and tonic in hand, reading a book and feeling warm ocean breezes blowing through my toes. It was paradise.

The next morning the Bass Queen and I were exploring the resort, finding the other restaurants and bars and shopping in the little shops on the resort. We wandered by one of the tour offices and they had a sign out. "Looking for one or two more fishermen," it said. We went in to investigate. The young man who ran the office told us that there were two other gentlemen that were looking for one or two more to share a fishing charter and to split the six hundred dollar cost.

The Bass Queen said "go for it" so I told him that I was interested. It took several phone calls until we finally got it all arranged. We met back at the tour office and each paid two hundred dollars. The two guys were buddies from Canada. One was an airline pilot and the other was a Canadian policeman. They had a rental car and we would leave the next morning at day break.

It was cool and windy the next morning as we got to the dock. But it was not nearly as cold as it would be if I were back in Minnesota. It was a satisfying feeling knowing that it was cold back home and I was going fishing on the ocean. But by Mexican standards it was chilly and I was glad to have a sweatshirt on. As our twenty eight foot boat cleared the harbor we turned into the Pacific Ocean. Now what doesn't seem to be a lot of wind while you are sitting on the beach is a lot different once you get on the ocean. We had six and eight foot waves around us and our boat seemed to get very tiny in that big ocean.

We ran about an hour out into the ocean before we stopped to start trolling. We had just finished getting out all the rods and had actually been fishing for only about fifteen minutes when one of the outriggers broke loose and the heavy trolling rod began to bounce. It was a marlin. The mate set the hook and handed the rod to the policeman. He had the fish on for about three minutes and then the fish was gone.

It seemed like a good start but this immediate spot of luck did not continue. It would be the one and only strike we would get. We spent the rest of the day getting beat up by the wind and waves, holding on tightly and trying not to lose our lunches.

By early afternoon we realized that our chances of catching anything was getting slimmer by the moment and that probably we were going to get back to the harbor without throwing up and counted ourselves lucky with that. Even some place as exotic as Mexico will have good days and bad days for fishing. Fishing is fishing is fishing. Even on the ocean, fishing can be a crapshoot and we had each just spent two hundred dollars on a boat ride.

Suddenly the captain and the mate started yelling and pointing out into the ocean. We climbed up on the bridge with them as the boat was slamming back and forth from the waves. We looked out to where they were pointing and we could see a fountain of water erupt from the ocean. It was a whale. We saw another spout. It was two whales.

The captain turned the boat towards them and we got closer. It was two sperm whales and we watched with awe as they came out of the water, breaching and twisting and turning before they would splash back into the water. We followed them for about half an hour. Neither whale seemed too concerned about us. Both of them were far larger than our little boat. They repeatedly breached the water. It was hard to believe something that big could do that like a bass flipping out the water on one of my lakes back home.

Eventually they dove and disappeared in the ocean. I had never seen anything like that in the wild before.

Although I am sure that our captain and mate had seen them before, they seemed just as fascinated as we were. I had to admit that it was the most inspiring sight that I have ever seen in nature. With that, my two hundred dollar boat ride without catching a fish seemed worth every penny.

AFTER THE RAIN

"Going fishing today?" Rita, our waitress, asked. At that moment it did not look promising. We were ordering breakfast at Al's Diner in Centuria, Wisconsin. Arnold, my fishing buddy from Germany, and I had seen the storm coming as we made the hour trip north from my home while dark, bruised, storm clouds gathered on the horizon.

It was just starting the initial sprinkle of rain as we parked the van. We had gotten through the first cup of coffee when Rita returned to get our order that the sky turned black, almost night like, and rain ran down the windows, splattering in puddles.

"We are hoping that it is going to stop by the time we finish breakfast," I said. She was too kind to make any comment on our sanity or lack of reality. It even seemed dark and gloomy inside the diner.

While we ate our ham and cheese omelets and hash browns it did not look good. Perhaps we were hoping for too much. Lightening flickered in the black, ugly sky and thunder boomed and rumbled and the rain pounded down while wind rattled the windows. This was one heck of a storm.

We kept ordering more coffee and delaying our departure in hopes that the weather would break. Just as the storm had started, it began to recede and by the time we were getting ready to pay the bill the rain was back to a sprinkle again.

"It does look like you guys will get some fishing in after all," Rita said as she took our money.

The last drops were coming down as we walked back across the parking lot. I pulled the plug and water poured out of the boat in a steady stream. Everything inside the boat was soaked.

The lake we wanted to fish was only a couple of miles away and by the time we got to the landing the rain had stopped completely. Water was still pouring out of the back of the boat. Although the rain had stopped, the skies were still gray and swirling overhead and it felt damp and cool and everything smelled refreshingly clean from the rain.

Water finally stopped running out of the boat. I put the plug back in as Arnold and I got the last things in the boat. As we pulled away from the dock it still didn't look real good but the sun did peek through the dull, gray clouds for just in instant as I had pushed the boat off the trailer into the water. I told Arnold that I did not know what the rain was going to do to the fishing but we might at least get a couple hours in before it starts to storm again. It seemed like a long way to drive for a just a couple of hours of fishing but it was the only thing we could do.

The wind began to pick up as we crossed the lake to the east shore. I dropped the trolling motor in and we began to flip crankbaits against the bank. Arnold quickly catches two bass and then I catch one. In the first half hour Arnold catches eight bass.

"I have never caught so many fish in such a short time," Arnold tells me.

It stayed that way for the next several hours. We kept steadily catching fish for the rest of the day. We lost count of the times that we both had fish on at the same time.

The fishing was so good that we stopped keeping track of the weather and eventually I noticed that the sun had come out and light blue skies replaced the dirty gray clouds we had earlier. I put on sunglasses.

No matter where we went on the lake we found fish. The lake is not particularly large with little less than three hundred acres and we had worked most of the shoreline with the trolling motor. By the time late afternoon arrived not only was it sunny, warm and humid as you would expect for a late summer day, but we had caught and released a bunch of fish. Most of our fish were bass with a handful of northern pike for a little extra excitement. Several of the bass went over three pounds.

Arnold had kept count of his fish and felt very satisfied when he caught fish number forty. On that particular milestone we stopped fishing. By now the sun was hot and the air was steamy from all the rain that we had earlier.

As I motored back to the landing Arnold told me that this is the most amount of fish he ever caught in one day. It was a great day of fishing and as we passed Al's Diner on our way home and I could not help but think of our eating breakfast there.

We weren't even sure that we were going to get out fishing at all then while being pounded by the storm. Who would have thought that we could have such a great day of fishing after the rain and Arnold would catch the most fish he ever caught in one day.

LESSONS FROM A FIVE YEAR OLD

Lessons on life and fishing sometimes come in the most unusual ways. Some many years ago I lived in Alabama where I learned to fish for bass. Bass fishing, like football, are not just mere past times or recreations in the land of hush puppies and grits. It is a way of life.

It was late fall day. Now late fall down south is far different than late fall up north. There isn't any ice or snow or cold weather. It was a bright warm day with gentle winds. The only way that you knew that it was fall was that the trees had turned color into the autumn hues.

My son Todd had turned five earlier in the year and was now beginning to go fishing with me in the boat. I wish I could say that I had a fancy bass boat in those days but I couldn't afford one then but I did have a fourteen foot jon boat with a trailer and a seven horse power motor.

One of the early lessons on fishing that I learned in Alabama was that fancy bass boats did not necessarily mean that you will catch more fish. You might be more comfortable while fishing in a fancy bass boat but it doesn't mean you will catch more fish. I caught a lot of fish from that cheap little jon boat while I lived Alabama.

But the jon boat had one major advantage over the bigger and fancy boats. I could fish a lot of smaller waters that those bass boats could never get into. One of those places was a small pond on a horse farm not far from my home. Through a series of personal relationships I had been given a standing invitation to fish it. The pond was less than a half acre and to get to it I had to drive through a horse corral into a horse pasture and across the earth dam that backed up the small stream that made the pond.

The pond was loaded with bass and bluegill that southerners called bream. I fished it in the spring and fall. During the summer, weeds choked the pond making it impossible to fish.

This late fall afternoon I was taking Todd on his first trip to the pond. It would be a good chance for him to get a big bass. Todd had a spincasting rod and I attached a floating Rapala to it.

I pulled the boat off the trailer and slid it into the water. I attached a transom mounted trolling motor to the boat and dragged the battery from my pick up truck down to the boat. I got Todd loaded into the front of the boat and we pushed off.

The trolling motor took us across the pond to the deep water against the earth dam. Trees grew along that stretch of shore and the deeper water and shade provided the best fishing on the pond.

I explained to Todd that he needed to cast his bait toward the shore where the fish would be and then we started fishing. Within about ten minutes I caught the first bass. As I unhooked the fish I noticed that Todd was fishing on the other side of the boat casting out toward the middle of the pond. I told him again that he needed to be casting toward the bank.

A little while later I caught another bass and again noticed that Todd was fishing the middle of the pond rather than the bank. I told him again to fish the bank because that was where the fish would be.

I was now starting to get irritated with Todd. He wasn't paying attention to what he was doing and wasting his efforts by just casting out toward the middle of the pond. He wasn't going to catch a fish by doing that.

I was about to say something again to him, this time a bit more strongly, when I began to wonder why I was getting upset. I wanted him to catch a bass and maybe a big bass but this seemed to be more important to me than it did to him. He was only five years old but he went fishing with me because he wanted to be with me and out in the boat. He was having fun doing what he was doing and wasn't a bit concerned.

I decided not to say anything. I caught another bass against the shore and Todd continued to cast out into the middle of the lake. Suddenly I heard him yell and I looked up to see his spincasting rod bent in half. Somewhere in the middle of the pond I heard a fish splash. I really wanted him to catch that fish and my heart flipped flopped each time the fish raced off. Within a minute or two Todd got the fish alongside the boat and I netted it. It was a three pound bass. Todd was a happy little fisherman.

An hour or so later we stopped fishing. I had caught five bass and Todd had caught only the one fish. But his was the biggest fish of the day.

Today Todd is now thirty years old. He is married and has a daughter. He owns his own business. We still fish together. Just a week ago he and I were fishing a small lake and we caught about forty bass.

I learned a few lessons about fishing that day from my five year old son. Sometimes fish will be in places you do not think that they are and just because someone is fishing different than you does not mean that they won't catch fish. But the most important lesson of all was about life. If someone is having fun doing what they are doing although it might be a little different, then what is wrong with that.

GRILLING IN WINTER

There once was a time that grilling had a regular season to it just like fishing season. When I was young, the grill came out of the garage on Memorial Day weekend. Sometimes, if it was a particularly warm spring the grill might come out of the corner behind the snow shovels a week or two earlier. However, for the most part, Memorial Day weekend signaled the beginning of the grilling season along with the semi official start of the summer.

Getting the grill out was the most anticipated event since at least Easter. It meant warm weather and lazy summer weekends that the family would all gather. My father and uncles would play horseshoes, drink beer and grill the meat. My Mother and aunts took care of potato salad, beans and the rest of the meal while trying to keep the kids away form the horse shoe pits so that one of us wouldn't get beaned with a horse shoe.

It was indeed a special event for father to grill out on a weekday. Generally if he did grill out on a weekday he probably was on vacation or maybe it was one of those steamy, hot, humid summer days when mother did not want to make the house any warmer by turning on the stove. You must remember few people had air conditioning then.

As summer would come to an end with the Labor Day weekend and school starting the next week it also meant the end of grilling season. There would be the last hamburger and bratwurst fry and perhaps one more grilled chicken dinner and that would be the end. The Tuesday after Labor Day us kids would get back on that yellow school bus for the first day of classes and Father would stick the grill back in the corner of the garage where it would sit until the next Memorial Day weekend.

It was fairly regimented society back in the 1950s and early 1960s. No one ever seemed to give any thought about how good a grilled bratwurst or steak might be for dinner on a cold winter evening. It just wasn't done.

But some people were beginning to break from the norm. One guy back in my hometown started to grill in the winter but of course it was much chillier to stand around the grill out in January then during the balmy days of July. So he decided to move the grill a little into the garage. He had taken all the seemingly prudent precautions of parking the car in the driveway and leaving the garage door open. One of his neighbors drove past one winter day while he was grilling and seeing smoke pouring out of his garage door called the fire department. His wife was especially embarrassed when all the fire trucks with the sirens blaring pulled into their driveway. As I recall that was the end of the husband's winter grilling for awhile.

But after living down south for a number of years I got used to grilling burgers and steaks and ribs and chicken in January and February as I did in June and July. Now living down south we did not have to put up with the snow and cold weather that those in the north had to endure so grilling in winter didn't seem so bad.

I had gotten used to grilling out all year long and when I was stationed in Germany with the U.S. Army I saw no reason to stop grilling in winter. We lived in government housing on base and had a top floor apartment with a balcony. Many of my neighbors thought it odd that I would be standing on my balcony during a snow storm, sipping a martini and cooking meat on the grill in January. It seemed perfectly normal to me.

Returning home to Wisconsin on leave, usually over Christmas, also required a bratwurst fry. I love bratwurst but until recently they were tough to find once you left the upper Midwest. So I had to get them when I came home. Although my father liked the grilled bratwurst, he thought I was a bit nuts so I would be standing outside in the snow grilling with temperatures dipping below zero while he watched from the inside. He did keep me supplied with martinis so that was alright.

I do have photos of one New Year's Eve when I was grilling bratwurst. It was a balmy winter evening when the temperatures were in the low twenties. All the guys came out to hangout around the grill, just like in summer. There was my brother, brother-in-law, my brother's father-in-law and even my father. The difference was that we were all bundled up in winter coats with caps over the ears and wearing mittens and gloves. Although my father joined the group around the grill I think he still thought we were nuts.

Since I moved back to the Midwest, retired from the Army and bought a home in Wisconsin, I have continued to grill all year long. Some people might think it nuts to be shoveling a path through the snow to the grill on the deck and putting on my ice fishing boots and winter jacket to grill a steak or some bratwurst and burgers but I do not.

If I am grilling on the deck in my backyard I do not have to worry about someone calling the fire department. My neighbors just think I am nuts.

There are times in the winter when a grilled steak or bratwurst and burgers taste even better than during the summer. You can always grill out in the summer but perhaps it is even more a treat when you have to shovel your way to the grill. If it is cold you just need to put more clothes on. So if it is nuts to grill out during the winter then I think it is a good nuts.

WISH BOOKS

Today they come right after Christmas. The first of the spring fishing catalogs seem to arrive about the time that I am throwing out the last of the wrapping paper and boxes left over from the Christmas presents.

I call them wish books and as the snow piles up outside around the house I can start to dream about spring, warmer weather and fishing. I now call them wish books because as I page through them I am wishing for spring and to be back on the water again.

But when I was a young fisherman I called them wish books because as I paged through them then I could only wish for most of the gear I saw. My meager summer grass cutting jobs required me to be frugal with my purchases.

Also as I recall from the days of my youth, the wish books came a bit later in the winter then they do now. Today we seem to rush the seasons. The mosquitoes are still attacking me when we are getting the first Christmas catalogs.

When I was growing up in the 1960s, the first fishing wish books did not arrive until about midwinter. It struck me then, as it does today, that it was good timing. By that time in the winter the really bitterly cold weather had settled in and it if wasn't cold it was snowing. Either way it discouraged any activity outdoors to include ice fishing.

It seemed when winter was at its most unbearable point the mail would bring some relief. The first wish books arrived. I would take them to my bedroom and at night when the freezing winds tugged at the corners of my parent's home I paged through them and marked an X on all the things I wanted. There would be a lot more Xs then what I would eventually order but on those winter nights it was time to dream.

Not only did those wish books set off dreams of stuff that I wanted to buy but launched far ranging dreams of places that I wanted to see and places that I wanted to fish. There would be the day, I told myself, that I would have all the fishing equipment that I wanted and I would fish waters far beyond my boyhood home.

In those days the wish books seemed to have more fishing stuff then non-fishing stuff in them. Today I do not think that is the case.

I remember when L.L. Bean and Eddie Bauer catalogs were for the serious outdoorsman and not catalogs for fashionable, upscale clothes. (To be fair, however, I should point out that L.L. Bean still does print an annual fishing catalog as well as a fall hunting catalog.) When I was a kid you could outfit yourself for a hunting expedition to Alaska with Eddie Bauer which probably you could not do today.

When it came to dreaming there was Orvis. They had the neatest fly fishing rods, reels and flies. They still have a catalog and you can order expensive fly rods from them. From a short list of remaining dreams, one day I will get an Orvis fly rod.

Then I wrote to Abercrombie & Fitch for one of their catalogs. That really set the dreams in motion. People who went on safaris, like Ernest Hemingway, shopped at Abercrombie & Fitch. I remember being in awe as I looked through that wish book. I should have kept that catalog but then again I wished too that I still had the shoebox of baseball cards I had then.

Gander Mountain had a wish book in those days. Today most people only know them because of the stores. Although they have been out of the wish book business for sometime Gander Mountain recently began to publish a catalog again. Then there was a company from the Midwest called Netcraft and you could not only get baits but lure and rod making supplies and all sorts of neat stuff you could putz with over the winter. They are still in business today.

But probably one of the greatest wish books of all time came from Minnesota. It was the Herter's catalog from Waseca. It was a big, robust wish book crammed with everything my youthful imagination could dream of. They billed themselves as being the authentic world source and I believed them. If Herter's said it was true it had to be true. I ordered from them often. The two most anticipated events in winter were when I got my annual Herter's catalog and when I got the order that I sent into them.

It has been thirty years since Herter's went out of business but I still have some of the gear I bought from them. I also still have two of their catalogs. They are as priceless as the memories they bring back. When I look through them, as I do every now and then, I am reminded of that young boy and the dreams that he had and am grateful for how many of those dreams came true.

Today we now have wish books from Bass Pro Shop and Cabela's. They seemed to take over after Herter's. I just got my first spring fishing wish books. I do not wish for as much stuff as I once did. I suppose that is because I have a basement full of fishing equipment. But when the cold winter winds whistle around the corners of my house I will still be wishing for spring while paging through today's wish books.

FIG NEWTONS

There are smells and tastes or sometimes just the mere mention of a certain food conjures up the memories of fishing trips from the past. For me, one of those foods is Fig Newtons.

The Fig Newton is a cookie made by Nabisco although I believe that others also make it. It has a wrapping of a soft cookie on the outside with a fig filling.

I first remember eating them while fishing with my father. My father traveled on his stomach. He was constantly eating. He always carried food with him. He had the most amazing metabolism of any person I have ever known. He never gained a pound no matter how much he ate.

Throughout his life he was six foot two inches and rail thin. I have a photo of him taken when he was in his 60's after he gave me his Marine Corps dress jacket that he wore home when he returned from World War II. I got him to put it on one more time for a photo and he still fit in his uniform that he had last worn forty years earlier.

I was never that lucky. I inherited a lot from my father but not his metabolism. Today I could not fit into any of my Army uniforms; not even the one I wore when I retired from the Army fourteen years ago.

When I fished with my father as a boy I too never worried about how much I ate or my weight. It finally caught up to me about the time I turned forty. However, in the days of my youth I was oblivious to those kinds of problems.

I have hundreds of vivid memories of fishing with my father but the one that comes to me every time I see a package of Fig Newtons is sitting in the front seat of one of his cars as we drove from one stream to another. Sometimes we never even bothered to take off our waders. He would be driving and we both would have a cup of coffee.

I thought that I was very grown up drinking a cup of coffee. But my youthful drinking of coffee was restricted only to fishing trips. It would usually be warm outside and the car windows were down. This was in the days before air conditioning in cars were standard features. I remembered the cars too. He had a 1961 brown Dodge and then later a 1965 white Mercury station wagon. The back of the car would be loaded with all of our fishing gear. The dust from dirt and gravel roads would be filtering in through the open windows. We would each have a cup of coffee in hand and a package of Fig Newtons sitting on the seat between us. We normally went through a package of Fig Newtons a day. If we were on a major fishing expedition we planned a package a day. It was always our between stream snack.

Eventually, as all children do, I grew up and left home. In my case it was to get married, go to school and eventually join the Army and made it a career.

I had forgotten about Fig Newtons. One day when I was a company commander of a basic training company in Alabama, the mess hall brought lunch out to the range where my company was firing. For dessert they had Fig Newtons.

My drill sergeants and I ate last after the troops and while we were eating before resuming training I told them about Fig Newtons and going trout fishing with my father. Apparently in the next couple of months the mess hall brought out Fig Newtons fairly regularly with lunch and I guess that each time I repeated that story of eating them while traveling to the next stream.

One day the mess hall brought Fig Newtons again and I started again on the story. I looked around and most of my drill sergeants had this glassy eyed look on their faces. They were too polite to say anything and then finally I said, "I guess I have told this story before." One them finally said, "Yes sir, you have."

So I stopped repeating the story after that and perhaps the mess hall stopped bringing them out. I forgot again about Fig Newtons until one day again after the noon mess hall vehicle had showed up on a range and trainees were sent over to help get the field mess set up. I turned around to see a young private standing behind me. He had a pained look on his face. Normally they do not want to talk to company commanders. He looked at me, thrust out a package of Fig Newtons and quickly said, "Drill Sergeant Harris sends this with his compliments."

The years have gone by and just recently I was in a grocery store and saw Fig Newtons. My seven year old grandson Max was visiting and we were going fishing. What a better time to try these again I thought as I bought them.

As it turned out, he wasn't impressed with Fig Newtons. Apparently it is an acquired taste and he had them once in day care and didn't like them. So I ate them myself and once again I was fourteen years old and fishing with my father, feeling very adult like by drinking coffee, sun beating through the windshield with the heat and dust coming through the windows rolled down on that 65 Mercury station wagon, eating Fig Newtons and looking forward to fishing on the next trout stream just down the road.

THE WINDS OF AUTUMN

A cold, biting wind came out of the north, ruffling the leaves and rippling the water of a small lake that we were fishing. The first bright red maple leaves are coming out and sumacs have turned a more subdued color of red wine. The shiny green trees that we saw for most of the summer now look washed out. The heat of summer has finally taken its toll, bleaching their colors and soon they will begin to change into their fall coats.

Above us gray clouds shift overhead and we hear the haunting call of a lone goose searching in the sky. We look up and finally pick it out high above in the swirling skies. The call of the goose and the occasional raucous screech of a crow are the only sounds that we hear. The woods are oddly quiet today as we hear no other animal or bird sounds.

Autumn is on its way. It is mid September but the cool winds for the first time today tell us that fall is on its way. Today we are wearing long pants and a shirt and a jacket. It is the first time that I have worn a jacket in what seems like a long time. The wind stings the cheeks and turns hands red. A couple of days earlier we fished in t-shirts and shorts like it was summer.

The winds of autumn in some ways seem refreshing after the hot scorching summer and drought. As much as I love the carefree days of summer, I always look forward to fall. It seems comfortable to put a blanket on the bed again and to have it cool enough to slip into a jacket during the day. The heat of summer is going away. No more air conditioning and fans blowing. Now we can leave the windows open again at night for the cool breezes that make us cover up.

Arnold and I are fishing a small lake near my home; an especially good lake for fall fishing. We are working tube jigs, slowly crawling them across the rocky bottom. The fish are hitting well this first day of the winds of autumn.

I feel a light bump on my line and then there is a sensation of weight where there wasn't before. I drop the rod tip, reel up the slack and then start to raise the rod tip again. The weight is still there. I pull back sharply to set the hook and there is little movement. The fish surges off and I turn it. The fish is alongside the boat and reaching over, I grab the fish and bring it in. It is a chunky, bright green largemouth. As cold as it is I find it strange to touch the fish and it still feels warm.

The water still holds the warmth of summer although the wind is cold. The first winds of fall will not immediately change the water temperature. But these cold winds are the beginning and soon the water temperatures will begin to decline as more of the trees change color.

As the afternoon goes on it becomes colder but we steadily catch fish. Arnold and I guess that we have caught and released over forty bass. It is a good day of fishing.

It will get colder and then all the leaves will turn color and drop. They will be scattered by the winds across the surface of the lake and hang up on treble hooks of crankbaits.

There will be days that it seems the only time that you don't get your crankbait back without a leaf speared on it will be if a fish hits it first.

It is the time for big fish. As I look back over the years most of my big fish were caught in the fall.

The days will become shorter and eventually ice will skim over the waters that I fish. The fishing season will come to an end but I won't worry about that for right now.

These first cool winds of autumn tell me that things are changing. I am looking forward to the changes and the adventures that come with it.

THE COMMISSIONER RULES

We were driving down from the mountains in North Carolina. The Bass Queen and I had spent several days in the mountains and were now on our way to Washington D.C.

We had spent our time visiting friends, watching the homecoming parade for the small college that I had taught ROTC at twenty years earlier and went fishing one day. It was a glorious fall day and the autumn colors were as bright as the sunlight.

The Bass Queen was driving. She was preoccupied. Finally she said "you need to call The Commissioner and get a ruling."

The day the before The Bass Queen and I were float fishing a river in Tennessee. This river is nationally known for its trout fishing. We were bobbing down the river in a small rubber pontoon boat. I sat in the front, our guide David rode in the middle, steering and rowing when needed, and The Bass Queen was perched on the rear seat.

We were fly fishing with tiny nymphs. I have fly fished for trout before but this was a new game for The Bass Queen. She has fly fished with me for bluegills and panfish but this was her first experience for trout.

I caught three or four trout when David steered our boat to the edge of a deep pool. He dropped a small anchor

183

that kept us from getting washed down any further on the river. I passed the fly rod to David who handed it to the Bass Queen. I took the camera and picked up my coffee cup. It was now her turn.

David explained to her that she needed to flip the fly line out into the rolling water, letting the strike indicator float across the deeper water. The strike indicator would dip when a fish hit and she needed to set the hook.

She missed the first fish and then the second and third. Finally she set the hook at the right moment and had a trout on for just an instant before she lost it. It was a frustrating experience for her.

She handed the rod back, took the camera and said that she would concentrate on taking photos instead. Although she would not try fishing again that day, she had a great time. We bobbed down the river and saw lots of spectacular scenery. David made us a wonderful shore lunch on an island in the middle of the river and we had lots of laughter and fun. I caught and released about two dozen trout that ranged from eight to sixteen inches and The Bass Queen took some stunning photos. It was a fun day.

What bothered her was if her brief few minutes of trout fishing would be considered getting skunked since she did not catch a fish. Now The Bass Queen takes getting skunked seriously. It has been several years since she last got skunked and she greatly prizes her record.

I picked up our cell phone and called. The Commissioner is my fishing buddy, Doug. He has been the arbitrator on many important fishing questions such as to what constitutes a skunk or if a fish can be counted as being caught and other weighty considerations.

I got him at work and advised him of the details.

"How long had she been fishing?" He asked.

"About fifteen minutes, no more than twenty," I told him.

I heard Doug briefly relate the situation to Ho Jo, who works with him. Finally he came back on the phone.

"If she was only fishing for that short period of time and she had never fly fished for trout before I think that it is like a preseason football game," he said. "No matter who wins or loses the game it doesn't count against the record. It is nothing more than a glorified practice. She wasn't skunked. Ho Jo agrees."

Obviously not only had he thoroughly deliberated over the circumstances of the situation but had gotten concurrence from a disinterested third party to validate his ruling.

As he hung up the phone I turned to The Bass Queen and told her "The Commissioner says that it doesn't count as a skunk."

The Bass Queen let out a sigh of relief.

THE ACCIDENTAL NORTHERN

I do not normally fish for northern pike. The exception to that is when I am in Canada. Typically we go out first for our dinner fish which is walleye. We fish jigs and cast or troll crankbaits for our food fish. In the course of fishing for walleyes we usually pick up our share of northerns as well which is ok.

I do admit that I enjoy the frenzied fight of a northern pike and I look at it as an added bonus to fishing for dinner. We even occasionally pick up some nice northern in the thirty plus inch sizes. Always exciting.

By early afternoon we return to camp, clean fish, drink a beer or two and then get out the heavier fishing gear. From then until just before dark we fish for big northern pike. Our goal is to catch a trophy northern which we have defined as any fish over forty inches.

Over the years we have caught a number of northern over thirty six inches. I have come tantalizingly close one time with fish that stretched to thirty nine inches, but nothing that broke forty. The trophy northern pike eluded me.

Back home I am primarily a bass fisherman, although I do fish for a little bit of everything. I will fish for panfish from time to time especially when I want to put a meal or two of fillets in the freezer. On a few days every year I will throw big baits for muskies. I will go after stream trout every now and then with both spinning and fly fishing equipment. In the early spring before the regular fishing season opens and later in the fall after the bass fishing slows down I will fish for walleyes in the Mississippi River. However, for most of the season I am bass fishing. I never fish specifically for northern pike.

I catch a number of northern pike every year while bass fishing. Bass and northern are generally found in much the same water so occasionally I will get a northern simply because they are there. Especially in the spring and early fall I will catch a few northern while bass fishing. Some of them are very good fish. One spring I caught a couple of fifteen pound northerns and a ten pounder in the first two weeks of the season.

I do not have anything against northern pike. I enjoy catching them when I do. They put up a great fight and they are always a bonus to a day of bass fishing. But with the exception of fishing in Canada I never bother to specifically fish for them.

A few years ago I was fishing with my then fourteen year old fishing buddy, Matt. It was a gray, cold, stormy late October day. We were looking for the last of the late season bass on a lake near my home. We had just started and I was casting a lipless crankbait toward a rocky bank that was close to deep water.

My bait stopped. My first thought was that I can't be hung up; there is nothing here. Then it dawned on me. This is a big fish. The fish surged off and the drag on my reel whined as it gave out line. The spinning rod was plunging and bent in half as the fish raced off.

I stopped the fish and turned it momentarily before it tore off again. After a few minutes I could see the fish in the water and when it swirled on top I could see that it was a big northern pike. A couple of minutes later I got the fish alongside the boat where Matt was holding out the net. The fish was a fat, heavy bodied thirty eight inch northern.

It was a great way to start the day. After releasing the fish Matt and I went back to bass fishing. We did catch some bass and although they all went between two and three pounds they did seem to be far and few between. Gray clouds swirled above us all day and temperatures stayed cold with a biting wind. Bass fishing was coming to a close for the year.

By the end of the afternoon we were fishing another rocky bank with deep water nearby when my bait stopped again. This time I immediately yelled out that it was a big fish. There was no doubt in my mind. The fish wouldn't budge initially and then burst off. My spinning rod was bent in half and the drag was making noises but it seemed to have little effect on the fish.

It splashed on top, making a swirl about the size of a bath tub. Each time I tried to get the fish to the boat it would race off again. I could feel the power of the fish all the way through the spinning rod. After several minutes I got the fish close enough that Matt was able to get the net under it but when he tried to lift it he was struggling. Dropping my rod, I grabbed the net handle and we both pulled the fish in as it twisted in the mesh.

The fish still had plenty of energy as I tried to wrestle the hooks out and stretch it out to measure it with a metal tape measure. It measured forty one inches and it was a fat fish from heavy fall feeding. I guessed that the fish probably went over twenty pounds. After photos I quickly slipped the fish back in the water and it never hesitated as it surged off.

After all the thousands of dollars I had spent in the last ten years and the trips to Canada trying to catch a trophy northern pike I would finally catch that fish while bass fishing half an hour from home. If I thought about it long enough there is probably a lesson there someplace.

THE JOHNSON SILVER MINNOW

It is one of the great baits of all time. It began in 1920 when Louis Johnson made the first spoons by cutting off the handles from table spoons and soldering a single hook to the underside. As the story goes, he liked the action from the baits but found that it collected a lot of weeds. He finally added a weed guard to it, making it like the Johnson Silver Minnow that we now see in our sporting goods stores.

The Johnson Silver Spoon caught on with fishermen from the very beginning. Fishermen had long realized that fish would be found in the weeds but until the Johnson Silver Spoon came along it was almost impossible to find a bait that could get through them without coming back with a mass of green stuff clinging to it.

It became popular with fishermen throughout the country because it worked. The spoon had a tantalizing side to side movement and the weed guard would keep weeds off the hook. The hook guard was strong enough to withstand countless numbers of fish that would bend the guard out of place when they slammed the baits. All a fisherman had to do was straighten it out, bend it back in place and it continued to work.

I have an old Silver Minnow that came from my grandfather's tackle box. I have no idea how old it is but it has "Pat'd 8-28-23" stamped into the underside of the bait. That was before my mother was born and she turns eight four in two weeks. This bait is beat up and scarred with some of the finish coming off. Although I would never use it because of the sentimental value, there is no doubt in my mind that I could catch fish with it today.

For anyone growing up in the 1950s and 60s like I did, the Johnson Silver Minnow was a main stay in any fisherman's tackle box. It was one of those baits that any serious fisherman just had to have; you never left home without it.

When I was a kid the Johnson Silver Minnow was my bait. My tackle box in those days was fairly meager. I had a few hooks and sinkers, a couple of bobbers, and two or three spoons and spinners. The only bait that I had more than one of was the Johnson Silver Minnow. The money I made from my small allowance and occasional grass cutting jobs did not allow me to spend much on fishing equipment. So I was going to invest it wisely on what I knew would work and that was the Silver Minnow.

I had three or four Silver Minnows and cherished them. Not only did they work but for me they represented, in those days, what seemed like a fairly sizable chunk of money. I sure did not want to lose any.

I used it all the time and caught a lot of fish with it. I caught walleyes and northern, smallmouth bass and white bass. Those where the main game fish in the waters near my boyhood home and I caught them all season long. I thought that there wasn't a better bait in the entire world.

But something happened in the late 1960s and early 70s. I stopped fishing the Johnson Silver Minnow. I do not know why. I was making a lot more money by then and perhaps I started buying newer baits and was succumbing to all the hype these other baits generated.

I had forgotten all about the Johnson Silver Minnow but on a trips to Canada some twenty years later I began to use them again for northern pike. They worked great, just like I remembered from the days of my youth. One of my fishing buddies casually wondered one day that if they worked so well on northern in Canada why wouldn't they work on bass back home.

Why wouldn't they, I thought. Later that summer I took one of those spoons out of my tackle box that I probably had not used in over twenty years and fished it on one of my home lakes. It was a warm, quiet summer night. Both bass and northern came rocketing out of the weeds to slam the Silver Minnow. I probably caught a dozen and a half fish in just a couple of hours and it made me wonder why I hadn't thought of trying it earlier.

When I was growing up the most popular Johnson Silver Minnow came in silver and was probably the first ones made, hence the name. But I do remember it also being in gold and black, however, silver was the only color for me. The Silver minnow now comes in a number of different colors including red and white and yellow and there are a number of imitations on the market today that have even more colors.

After some experimentation I have found that the original Johnson Silver Minnow in their primary three colors seems to still work the best. One evening, my neighbors, Jeff and Lisa fished with me using the Silver Minnow. I took the black and Jeff and Lisa took the silver and gold. The Silver Minnow coaxed the fish from the weeds. They hit hard and we saw them flash in the clear water as they struck. All three colors caught fish without one color doing any better than the other.

The Johnson Silver Minnow has stood the test of time. It has been catching fish for almost ninety years. New baits come and go but some, like the Johnson Silver Minnow, will always catch fish. I guess that there is something to be said for sticking to something that you know works.

PIGS IN A CAN

I was once in a sports store and talking to a fellow bass fisherman. He asked me, "Do you have pigs in a can?"

I had no idea what this fellow was talking about but I thought perhaps this was some hot shot new bait that I should have known about and I did not want to seem ignorant. He mentioned pigs in a can several more times in our conversation and then it dawned on me. He was talking about pork such as the Uncle Josh pork frogs and strips.

Where ever did this guy hear that expression? I have never heard of anyone ever calling pork, pigs in a can and have never heard anyone refer to it that way again. But since Uncle Josh first started making pork frogs in the 1920s I suppose there have been a number of unique nicknames for them.

I am sure that there are other companies that make pork frog and strips and those types of baits. However, it is Uncle Josh that first made them and is certainly the company that is best known for them. Two young fishermen, Alan P. Jones and his fishing buddy Urban Schreiner had been fishing Jordan Lake in Adams County near Oxford, Wisconsin. After Alan had gotten out of the Navy at the end of World

War I, he and Urban made yearly trips to Jordan Lake for bass fishing.

They fished plugs in the morning and in the afternoon switched to live frogs and caught lots of bass all day long. But during their fishing trip in 1920 they could not find any frogs. Apparently their bass catching diminished significantly with the lack of frogs. They needed something else; which is always the impetus to new discoveries.

So the two young fishermen went into Oxford to a butcher shop and bought hunks of fat back. Back at the lake they whittled and carved on the fat back something that resembled a frog. With that they went out and caught a bunch of bass. A new bait was born.

Alan's family owned the Jones Dairy Farm where they raised pigs for sausage that was nationally known. Once he returned back home he had lots of pork hides and fat back to work with. By 1922 they began commercial production of their baits. The new baits were an instant hit with fishermen. They initially offered only frogs and strips which probably is still their most popular baits. In the early days their baits only came in white and green.

The name Uncle Josh came from the guy who owned the farm and rented them boats on Lake Jordan. He sounded like a popular comedian of the day named Uncle Josh so they hung the nickname on him. Once the company started, they liked the name and put it on their baits. Their jar of baits still has the figure of Uncle Josh with a pipe clamped in his mouth. The company was in Fort Atkinson, Wisconsin and is still there today.

One of their first big orders was for $300 from a company called Jenny-Semple-Hill in Minneapolis. After World War II new dyes allowed them to provide more colors and they added more shapes and styles of baits to what we know today.

During the days of my youth during the 1950s and 60s every fisherman I knew had a jar or two of Uncle Josh pork frogs or strips in their tackle box. The jars in those days were made of glass. Sometimes the salty brine that the pork came in corroded on the lid, making it difficult to open. Having a pliers in your tackle box came in handy in many ways to include making it easier to get the lids off jars of Uncle Josh. Most fishermen's tackle box had a bit of dried salt brine crusted on the bottom but no one really noticed too much. The bait was the important thing.

Both my grandfather and father had a jar or two of Uncle Josh rolling around their tackle boxes. There were any number of artificials that could work with Uncle Josh but probably spoons were the most popular especially the Johnson Silver Minnow. If you fished for northern pike or bass you always used the Silver Minnow around weeds with an Uncle Josh pork frog or strip.

But as time has gone on the world of plastics has invaded bass fishing. But Uncle Josh held it's own. Plastics are good but a bass strip of Uncle Josh still has more action than any plastic bait I have seen.

I still use Uncle Josh. For a blast from the past that still catches fish today, try a Johnson Silver Minnow with a white or yellow bass strip. A bass strip would be a great trailer on a spinner bait. The pig and jig has been around bass fishing for over thirty plus years and although there are all sorts of plastic frogs on the market today they still do not have the same stimulating action as a pork frog. For those who use scents, pork frogs will soak up more scent and it will last longer with pork then most plastic products.

Just like my grandfather and father I have several jars of Uncle Josh baits floating around my boat and it still catches fish just like it did for them. With all the innovations and new baits in today's fishing, some things, like Uncle Josh, will never change. If it has been working for almost ninety years then why fix what is not broke.

As my fishing buddy Scott said "pork isn't just for politicians anymore." But I will never call it pigs in a can.

GOING NORTH

The big question for the last week has been, "Where are you going for the opener?" This is a much discussed subject among us fishermen. Serious stuff; the opener can't be taken lightly.

For me there is no question where I will be. I will be at Cut Foot Sioux. We stay at a cabin called Drakes Hideaway sitting on the shores of the lake.

It is an eclectic group that gathers there. The elders of the group are Reed and The Judge. Then there is a bunch of us middle age guys, several which are now bringing sons along. Counting the kids, there is usually about a dozen and a half fishermen there for the opener.

Traditions abound here. The cabin was originally purchased by six guys half a century ago. Reed is the only one that remains from the original six. The Judge also came along in the very early years. Most of the middle age guys first came to Drakes Hideaway as kids themselves, being brought there by their fathers. Now they bring their sons.

Just being there is as important as the fishing. Some years we catch lots of fish on The Opener. Other years we don't. But it really doesn't matter. Every year we have lots of fun, there is laughter and stories told, memories recalled and good food eaten.

The food itself is worth the trip. On Friday we have hamburgers. Now these are not the little floppy things you find at a fast food restaurant. These burgers are thick and juicy made on the grill over charcoal. On Saturday night we have steaks. One year the steaks were so thick that they were each like a small roast. For breakfast there is eggs, bacon one morning and sausage the next, fried potatoes, a mound of toast and gallons of coffee. Lunch is home made beans and sandwiches. For dessert there are pies that The Judge's wife sends and The Bass Queen's cheese cakes. Oh yes, in the evenings when the fishing is done occasionally there is a nip on the liquor bottle.

There is not a better place in the whole world to be at for The Opener in Minnesota than at Drakes Hideaway.

So for the last week every time someone asks me where I will be at for the opener the excitement builds. Also during this last week are all the final preparations. Rods and reels are checked. I go through the tackle box to make sure that I have the right jigs. I get the sleeping bag down and pack a bag with all the clothes that I need and I pack a lot of heavy clothes because it will be cold.

On the Thursday before I pack the van. I put in a couple of jig rods, a couple of bait rig rods and a couple of trolling rods. I have the tackle box with the jigs and bait rigs and another one for trolling baits. In all the years that I have been coming up there we have only trolled a couple of times but I still bring the trolling gear along. I would hate to be there and need it and not have it. The Bass Queen is making her cheese cakes for me to take along. Reed told me once not to bother coming up there if I did not bring them.

The next morning the last thing I pack is the cheese cakes. I hook up the boat to the van and pull out of the driveway. Going around and through the Twin Cities is usually a pain, especially while dragging a boat. Once I get out of all the traffic I begin to relax. I am going fishing.

As I drive north on Highway 35 I watch as the land begins to change. Farms and fields begin to drop away and then there are more woods. With all these changes I get a little more excited. I pop a CD in and the sounds of Willie Nelson come out. I have put in some thought as to what to listen to on the way north and Willie Nelson seems particularly fitting. Traffic is heavier than normal and most of the cars seem to be towing boats.

I turn off on Highway 73. The road twists and turns more and I start to see an occasional lake. At Cromwell I stop at a gas station to use the rest room, get a soda and a candy bar. It is the same every year. It is part of the routine. It is the same gas station and the same brand of soda and candy bar. I pass one lake that tempts me. It looks bassy and I say to myself that later in the month when the bass season opens I want to come back.

Then I get to highway 2. There are long caravans of cars and trucks pulling boats. Those few cars that are not towing boats probably are filled with other fishermen. You can feel the excitement in the air now. We all seem to be one large traveling community of walleye fishermen.

I get to Grand Rapids and stop to get bait. The town is bubbling with excitement and anticipation. "How do you think it will be tomorrow?" That question is asked time and time again. I get a couple of plastic bags of minnows; one for chubs and the other of shiners, and a couple of containers of night crawlers. I also get more jigs. You can never have too many. Every gas station, bait shop and liquor store in town has cars with boats driving in and out of their parking lot.

Now I turn off the CD player for the last few miles. I like the sound of silence as I am driving through the towering pines. I am almost there and I am savoring it. Then I turnoff the road onto a dirt road with a cloud of dust trailing behind the boat as I am driving.

I am finally there. I get out of the car and breathe in the clear, cool, fresh air. I am met by Reed. We shake hands and he asks if I brought the cheese cakes. I know that I have arrived.

IF IT ISN'T SNOWING ITS . . .

Whether or not the fish are hitting is always the biggest mystery of The Opener. But the second biggest mystery is what the weather will be like. I am not sure that anyone really needs to ask that question. It will be snowing.

In fact, if it isn't snowing would it really be The Opener in Minnesota? I think not.

I suppose that might depend on where you fish on The Opener. If you fish in the southern part of the state the weather may be different then if you fish in the far north. In my case I pose the question based upon where I will be fishing.

I fish at only one place for The Opener and that is at Cut Foot Sioux in the far northern part of the state. I have been going there for several years and it just seems to me that every Opener that I have been on that lake it has snowed.

One year when I left the Twin Cities it was warm and sunny. I was wearing a short sleeve shirt when I left home and it seemed comfortable enough as I drove north. Four hours later, when I arrived at a place called Drakes Hideaway, a cabin on the shores of Cut Foot Sioux; it was starting to get a bit chilly. But then it was dark by that time and I expected that it might be getting colder.

The next morning I awoke and went out into the kitchen to get a cup of coffee. As I looked outside I saw that it was snowing. Now, this was no mere flurries. This was a full fledged raging blizzard. In addition to the snow a bitingly cold, roaring wind whipped the lake into whitecaps and battered the boats tied to the dock. It was a typical opener.

I suppose that there have been times when it did not snow and I believe that I have been on a couple of those. But I don't remember those as well as when it snowed. Perhaps it is because it has snowed more often than not on the opener and I just expect it now. It just wouldn't be The Opener if it wasn't snowing.

I even plan for it now. In one of the early years I was packing the night before leaving for the opener and when I got all finished my wife, The Bass Queen said "Humor me. Take along your down jacket." It was a bright, warm day and although I knew that I would be traveling four hours north yet, could the weather change that radically? It did and I was ever so glad that I had listened to the Bass Queen. Yep, it started to snow shortly after we got out on the lake Saturday morning. The wind picked up and even with the down jacket I was cold but I would have been a lot colder if I did not have it.

One year when Dennis and I first got out on the lake I noticed that it wasn't too cold and the winds were light. We had gray skies above but it seemed downright balmy by most opening day standards. I pointed out to Dennis that it wasn't snowing.

He looked up at the skies and said, "Not yet." Dennis grew up in Grand Rapids and is part owner of Drakes Hideaway. He has been there for a lot of Openers. Dennis knows better than to be too optimistic about the weather for The Opener.

We got through the whole morning without snow and even for a couple of hours after lunch. About mid afternoon the temperatures dropped, the wind howled out of the north and the gray skies started to spit snow.

"It was only a matter of time, wasn't it?" I asked Dennis. He just nodded. He had been there too many times before.

But the good thing about when it snows on The Opener is that it has no adverse effect on the fishing. In fact, I believe it makes the fishing even better. The couple of times it did not snow on The Opener I do not recall getting many fish. However, on the days that it snowed we seem to always catch fish. In that case I will take the snow every time.

Last year was a prime example. As we were sipping coffee in the cabin just before going out it was sunny. Temperatures were a bit chilly but that was alright. Dennis, The Judge and I went out. We immediately started catching fish. By the time we went in for a late breakfast we had caught and released five fish that ranged from seventeen and a half inches to a twenty two inch walleye The Judge caught, the biggest fish of the morning.

As we were out there the wind started to pick up. That usually means that something is going to change. The blue skies disappeared, replaced by lead gray clouds. Later in the afternoon when we went back out it was cold and then it started to snow. I was expecting it. Wind battered us and the snow fell heavily and at times obscured the shore. But we still were catching fish and I caught a twenty five inch walleye. It was turning into a great day of fishing.

At one point we were drifting by Reed and his son Scott in Scott's boat.

"It wouldn't be The Opener if it wasn't snowing," I said.

Scott looked up at the snow for a moment and then said, "It is beautiful."

It snowed for the rest of the afternoon and early evening and was still snowing while I was grilling out steaks. Reed, who along with The Judge are the camp elders, said it was the best Opening Day he could remember. Reed was one of the original six owners who bought Drakes Hideaway fifty years ago so he has seen his share of openers. If he says that it was the best Opener he could remember then all that I can say is let it snow.

ONLY WALLEYE

We were launching our boat when we saw a boat with two fishermen pull up to the other side of the dock.

"How did you guys do?" I asked as I pushed the boat off the trailer, sliding it into the water.

"We did ok," the one guy said. "We got a couple of walleyes."

I looked out on the lake and the landing was on a small bay that was ringed with lily pads. It looked to me like there should be some bass out there.

"Any bass in this lake?" I asked.

These two guys immediately got a pained look on their faces like I had just told them that someone stole their truck.

"Bass?" One of the guys asked.

"Ya, bass." I said. "Are there any bass out there?"

They looked at each other in amazement. They were incredulous that any one would even care if bass were in that lake. You could see them saying to each other "Is that like carp or something?"

Finally one of the guys said, "Well, I guess so." I am sure they were thinking why would anyone want to fish for bass when you have walleyes. They looked at me like there had to be something the matter with me. I am sure that they were saying to themselves, "This guy needs professional help."

The Bass Queen and I pulled away from the dock and I thought we would just give the lily pads a quick try to see if anything was in them.

Within the first few casts we both had fish. For the next several hours we steadily caught bass and never left the bay. The water was clear and we could see the fish coming out of the lily pads to attack our baits. It was a great afternoon of fishing and by the end we had caught and released about three dozen bass.

Although the bass fishing had been good I realized that there are people, like the guys we met as we were launching, that believe that there is only one fish worth fishing for. That would be walleyes. If it isn't walleye it just isn't worth your time. Friends do not let friends fish for anything else but walleyes.

This attitude is fairly prevalent throughout northern Minnesota and Wisconsin. Those two guys at the boat landing could not understand why anyone would want to fish for bass. I could have told them that I was fishing for carp or bullheads and I would have gotten the same response from them.

Now I will be the first to admit that when it comes to eating fish it is hard to beat walleye. I can't remember when the last time I ate bass and probably will never eat another one. But I do love to eat walleye so when it comes to getting eating fish I fish for walleyes.

Being primarily a bass fisherman, however, I do fish for walleyes off and on throughout the year. In the early spring before the normal fishing season opens and later in the fall when the bass fishing slows down I fish for walleye on the Mississippi River. During the heat of the summer I will troll in the evenings on the Mississippi River for walleyes. I have been going to Canada for years and I fish for walleyes there. For the Minnesota opener and for a weekend in the fall that we call The Fall Classic I fish for walleyes on Cut Foot Sioux.

I stay at a cabin called Drakes Hideaway thanks to the invitation of an old Army and fishing buddy, Dennis. Reed and another long time member, The Judge, are the elders of Drakes Hideaway. Reed has left his imprint on Drakes Hideaway in so many ways but none as indelibly as his attitude toward the walleye. He once told me that if isn't walleye all other fish are either bait fish or trash fish.

There are other fish in Cut Foot Sioux besides walleye. There are northern pike, big perch and crappies as well as others. We seldom bring any of those other fish back to the cabin. To do so earns Reed's disdain. Dennis told me that when he was a kid, fishing at Drakes Hideaway, that they would catch some big northern but no matter how big those fish might be Reed looked at them with absolute contempt. So when I fish up there I only keep walleyes because nothing else is worth fishing for.

One year I stopped at a bait shop in Grand Rapids on my way to Cut Foot Sioux for The Fall Classic. I asked about the walleyes and one of the guys in the store said he hadn't heard anything about the walleye but he knew some guys were catching some nice crappies there.

I looked at him in shock and told him, "We fish for walleyes; all other fish are either bait fish or trash fish." The guy looked at me like I was demented. I smiled at him with a smug look on my face and walked out. Reed would have been so proud.

SUMMER COLD

It just doesn't seem right; getting a cold in summer. It is hot and sunny and everyone wants to be outside. Winter is an ok time to get a cold. It is nasty outside anyway so there is a natural inclination to stay indoors and nurse your cold until it is gone.

But in summer it is a different case. The summer weather that begs you to come outside seems to make the aches and pains of a cold all that much worse.

It is the middle of summer and I have a cold. The Bass Queen got it first and then I caught it. However, as summer colds go mine was not too bad. My voice became raspy making it difficult to talk. I am sure some people felt that was all together not a bad thing for me. My sinuses opened up a like a spring accompanied by a nagging cough. Luckily, I did not have the headaches and fever and body aches that make you feel that you had been worked over with a baseball bat. At least I could sleep at night which is alright when you have a cold.

But the cold is one of those things that is a major irritant; making life all around unpleasant. I was going through a lot of hankies and Kleenex, gobbling aspirin and generally moping around a lot.

Then Scott called me.

"You do not sound so hot," he said.

"I'm ok," I gasped.

"You want to go fishing?" He asked.

"Ya," I said. My voice was not allowing me to get into lengthy discussions. It would start out raspy and within a sentence or two disintegrate into only croaks. I was saving my voice for only the most essential communications. By the time we had determined what time I was to pick him up and what lake we were going to fish I was voiceless.

I waited until some of my voice had came back before calling The Bass Queen to telling here that Scott and I were going fishing.

"I don't think that is wise with your cold," she offered. I suggested between coughs that what could be better for a cold then fresh air and sunshine and if I am going to be getting fresh air and sunshine then I might as well be fishing. She reluctantly agreed with my logic.

On the way to the lake Scott talked about sports and fishing and those types of things that guys talk about when going fishing. I gasped, coughed and croaked.

I started to feel considerably better as soon as we pushed the boat off the trailer into the water. Scott had fished this lake a few days earlier and suggested that we start on a small point a little way down the lake. I just nodded. A short discussion about baseball had robbed me of my voice.

We were flipping plastic worms into shallow water and working them back into deeper water. We were at it for about ten minutes when I felt a light tap. Dropping the rod tip I waited for a moment and could still feel pressure on the line when I pulled back to set the hook. The fish hesitated for a moment and then tore off and my drag began to whine. I am not sure that there is a better sound then the noise a drag makes as a fish is pulling line off your reel.

The fish turned out to be a fifteen inch largemouth. A few minutes later I caught another fish and then Scott caught a bass. This sun and fresh air was doing wonders for my cold. Catching fish helped too. I was starting to feel much better.

As the afternoon wore on we continued to catch fish. We did not catch a lot of fish but the fish we were getting were all over fourteen inches. This might be the best medicine for a cold, I thought to myself.

I flipped my worm back into a shallow pocket. As soon as the worm splashed into the water I felt a fish slam it and the line tighten. I set the hook and for an instant thought I had pulled the hook out of the fish and sunk it into a log. I pulled back on the rod to dislodge the hook and then felt the thumping of a fish.

"This is a big fish," I croaked. I was initially concerned because the fish was in shallow water with a lot of tree stumps and I did not know if I could pull the fish out. My drag was making noises but I kept the pressure on the fish and with lots of splashing I finally forced the fish into deeper water where there was a lot less wood for it to get tangled in.

The fish put up a hard fought battle but eventually I got it alongside the boat and reached over, grabbed the fish and brought it in. It was a twenty inch bass that probably went about five and a half pounds. After pulling the hook out and taking a quick photo, I released the fish.

By late afternoon when we decided to go home, Scott and I had caught over a dozen big bass. I was feeling much better. Although my voice was still raspy and hoarse, the rest of my cold seemed well on the mend.

I thought to myself that there really is something about sunshine and warm weather and catching bass that makes for good medicine. Perhaps I might need to write this up for one of those medical journals.

FASHION UPDATE

Well, I started wearing the pith helmet this fishing season. I got only minimally weird looks from other fishermen. When I ran into my fishing buddy, Jerry, I was wearing my pith helmet and I asked him what he thought of it.

He looked quizzically at me for a moment and then said, "I am not sure what to say." I will take that as a positive reaction.

During the sunniest days of the summer I found the pith helmet to be an ideal fishing hat. It provided wrap around shade that coved my neck and ears as well as my face. Very functional. It kept me cooler than a regular baseball cap and that is always good.

I found another advantage to the pith helmet when I was fishing with a couple of young boys one weekend this summer. One of the boys was standing next to me in my boat when he cocked his arm to cast. As he brought the bait forward he bounced it off the side of my pith helmet. I think if I wasn't wearing that pith helmet the hook would have imbedded itself into the side of my head. That would not have been good.

I would occasionally wear those fancy nylon fishing shirts with all the pockets but I went back to my t-shirts.

At least The Bass Queen got rid of all the t-shirts that had holes in them so I did not look too scruffy.

One morning I picked up my fishing buddy, Scott. He looked like he had just stepped out of a sports catalog photo shoot. He wore nylon zip off fishing pants and a matching color coordinated nylon, short sleeved shirt that bristled with pockets.

"Boy do you look spiffy," I said.

He looked at me with disdain as I walked up to him wearing my t-shirt.

"You never will learn, will you," he said. "My wife bought this for me for Father's Day. She told me to wear this the next time I went fishing with you."

"What do you do with all the pockets?" I asked.

"I don't know but it does look a lot better than a t-shirt," he said.

We loaded all his gear into my boat and we left. We drove to a lake further north than we normally go. We stopped once at a small deli, gas station, country store to pick up sandwiches and then got to the lake.

As we were getting the boat ready he looked critically at me again.

"Do you know that you are wearing your t-shirt inside out?" He asked.

I looked down. Sure enough.

"No I didn't," I said as I pulled my shirt off to turn it right side out.

"You know," he said. "You got to look right to catch fish."

BILL AND MIKE'S EXCELLENT ADVENTURE

Bill and I have been friends since high school. Since our graduating class just held our fortieth class reunion it gives you some idea how long that has been.

We have had our share of adventures and misadventures over the years. When we were younger we probably had more misadventures than adventures and now that we are older we tend to have more adventures than misadventures. I guess that is the nature of getting old.

In the days of our youth we drank a little beer, chased girls and wrecked havoc on our father's cars. Sometime we did have a bit too much fun. Bill's father, who I called Mister Dad, once told my wife that when we were young he "would not have given a plug nickel for the two of us."

Now Bill and I are rapidly approaching the age when we can start drawing social security. It is hard to believe. What happened to all those years? Bill and I both married, actually started careers, had kids, bought a house and now even have grandbabies.

We got respectable. Mister Dad was pleasantly surprised that Bill and I made it to adulthood and was even more amazed that we became responsible members of society.

Now that Bill and I have become mature, although our wives might beg to differ with that, he and I still get together periodically. We tip a glass or two, smoke a cigar, reminisce about our misspent youth, put some meat on the grill, and go fishing.

Earlier this year Bill and his wife Karen came to visit. We left our wives on the deck at our house and Bill and I headed for the lake. It was a grand and glorious day with blue skies, fluffy white clouds and warm breezes.

We were catching a few bass to keep us busy, catching up on what our kids and grandkids were doing and remembering some of our misadventures. We were laughing and talking and catching some fish and had not been paying much attention to anything else. We were taken completely by surprise when a boat that we were passing pointed out that the sky behind us was starting to look ugly. We turned around and they were right. Black clouds were swirling around behind us.

We took note of the sky but continued to fish. We worked through another bay and then noticed that the dark, storm clouds were taking over the sky, the temperature started to fall and the wind picked up. I suggested that perhaps we might head back to the landing. Bill agreed. Our wives would have been so proud of our prudence.

Our timing was not good, however. We had waited a bit too long. It started to sprinkle by the time we pulled up to the landing. Bill went to get the van but by the time he was backing the trailer into the water the skies opened up, pouring down rain. I ran the boat up on the trailer and Bill hooked up the boat and pulled us out.

He drove a couple of hundred yards and stopped. I jumped down to help get the straps on the boat when I noticed that two of the rollers had flipped up getting caught underneath the boat. We needed to back the boat back in, float the boat off the trailer and hopefully the rollers would flip back to where they were supposed to be. We tried it again and when we pulled the boat back out, the rollers were still in the wrong position. By this time Bill and I were both drenched, shirts and shorts soaked and clinging to our bodies.

We realized that this was not going to work and we were just getting wetter. We quickly strapped the boat down the way it was, pulled off our soggy shirts and left. As we were pulling away and the rain was pounding on the van I asked Bill if he remembered that time that he, his dad and I were fishing on Deer Lake and as we were trying to beat a storm back to the boat landing ran out of gas. I had another tank in the boat but we got drenched before I could switch tanks and get the motor started again. He said he did and we laughed at the memory.

Seven miles down the road it suddenly stopped raining. Doesn't it always happen like that? I told Bill that I knew of a little lake not too far away and suggested that we stop there on our way home, launch the boat again, and quickly fix the roller problem. Bill said it sounded like a good idea. By that time it was blue skies and warm again.

To my surprise, when we got to the landing there was hardly anyone there although it normally is a very popular lake. I found a couple of sweatshirts in the back of the van and we put them on and started to feel almost dry. We launched the boat and I flipped over the rollers. I looked around for a moment. "What the heck," I said. "Let's go fishing." The boat was in the water, we were relatively dry, and it was sunny again so off we went.

We fished until dark, ended up catching a bunch more bass and laughed again at some of our youthful escapades. It was another most excellent adventure.

RAIN GEAR

It is one of those indispensable things. If you spend anytime in the outdoors you need it. Over the years I have worn countless types of rain gear which has gone on to perpetuate a long standing love hate relationship with the stuff.

One of the first things I began to realize about rain gear is that waterproof is a relative concept. I understand that nothing you are going to wear is going to be one hundred percent waterproof.

I haven't found anything yet that works completely. There is nothing like an all day soaker to test out a set of rain gear. Spend a rainy day in a boat and you will find all the places that water can leak in. Around the neck is a case in point. Rain gear never seems to have a good seal around the neck and after spending the day in the rain usually my shoulders, upper chest and upper back will be wet. I consider it a successful day when those areas are just damp but all too often I am soaked.

Age takes its toll on waterproofing. It seems just that when you get to the point that your rain gear becomes comfortable to wear after a couple of years, it starts to seep water in other places. Seams in the clothing are usually the first places that start to leak.

If the weather is hot, wearing rain gear can be especially annoying. There are times in the summer that I put on rain gear and an hour or so later, when the rain has stopped, I find that I am just as wet from sweating inside of it as I would be if I had not worn it all.

I do not care for hoods. Yes I know that there are days that you really do need to pull up the hoods during a heavy drencher and I do then but I really do not like it. I find hoods to be so claustrophobic. Once you pull up the hood you can only see right in front of you through the hole in the hood. I know that you stay drier that way but you sure can't see much around you. It then requires you to move your whole body so that you can see. If you turn your head all you see is the inside of the hood. If there are two of you in the boat it is almost impossible to talk since all your senses are blocked off and if you are trying to communicate you seem to be yelling out at each other from underneath the hood.

The real secret to wearing rain gear is to put it on before you get wet. I seem to never be real good at timing that. Since I do not care to wear rain gear all that often, once it does start to rain I am reluctant to stop fishing and put it on. Not only am I interrupting my fishing but then I have to scrounge around in one of the boat lockers until I finally do get the rain gear out. Usually it is always under a ton of other stuff like extra tackle, a tool box, life vest, ropes, etc. and of course the rain gear is always on the very bottom.

Now by the time I actually get the rain gear out everything else in the locker is piled on the floor of the boat and getting wet. Why can't it rain when my rain gear is on the top of all that stuff so that all I have to do is just open up the locker and grab it? This I will never know. There have been times that it has stopped raining by the time that

I have finally found my rain gear. Of course by this time I am soaked.

I have also noticed that it seems to rain harder when you are not wearing your rain gear. Because I am hesitant to put on rain gear to start with I generally always wait until I am wet before I finally get it on. It is only going to rain for just a bit and it will be done in a minute or two, I say to myself.

By the time I have realized that this is not the case and I had better put my rain gear on I am now saturated. So when I finally do get the rain gear on inevitably it will stop raining shortly thereafter. The best way to insure that it will rain longer and harder is for me to not put my rain gear on and the best way to make it stop raining is for me to put it on. This has happened to me so often that I think that this is a law of nature.

However, every now and then and this does not seem to happen often, I actually do call it right. It starts to sprinkle a little bit. I look off in the distance and see nothing but dark, ugly rain clouds coming our way. I suggest to my fishing partner that we better get our rain gear on. We get it out, pull on our rain gear and a few minutes later it begins a steady and relentless downpour. I am feeling ever so clever and satisfied. I got it right.

Then I notice that my rain gear is leaking and I can feel the water soaking into my dry clothes. I guess that I will never win at this.

BIKES

I saw something the other day that I rarely see today. I saw two boys riding bikes. It occurred to me that in the normal course of any given week I see a lot more adults riding bikes for exercise then I see kids riding bikes as their normal means of transportation.

What made it seem all the more unusual was that both of the boys were carrying fishing rods. I can not tell you when was the last time I saw any boy riding a bike with a fishing rod in hand on his way to a fishing hole.

There was a time back in the 1950s and 60s, when if you were a kid, the only way you were ever going to get around was on a bike. Parents did not feel especially obligated to cart kids around in the family car. If you were a kid and you wanted to go someplace you rode your bike. That was all that there was to it.

This was of course in the days prior to organized baseball, soccer and other structured extracurricular activities for kids. Especially in the summer, if you wanted to play baseball you got a few kids together from the neighborhood, got the bat and baseball out from the basement or garage and you played your game in someone's backyard. Everyone rode over on their bikes. Bases were trees or bushes and after the game, if you were lucky, the mother of the kid hosting the game would come out with a pitcher of Kool-Aid. It wasn't complicated.

It was the same if you wanted to go fishing. The fishing trip usually commenced with getting bait. Most of our kid fishing was with live bait; primarily worms or night crawlers. We normally did not have many baits with the exception of perhaps an odd red and white or silver spoon and maybe a spinner or two. Plugs, that we now call crankbaits, were way too expensive for kids. Tackle boxes were fairly basic then. It normally consisted of a few hooks, sinkers and a couple of bobbers.

Collecting live bait normally happened in one of two ways. The night before, after dark, you would tread cautiously across the lawn with a flashlight in hand, grabbing night crawlers off the grass or on the morning of the fishing expedition you would go out to the garden and dig up a bunch of worms. Either way your bait would then be placed in a tin can and covered with dirt. This was in the days before aluminum cans and your tin can was as essential a part of fishing as your rod and reel.

Most of us only had one rod and reel. Normally it was a spincasting rod. There were any number of cheap spincasting combinations on the market back then but if you were really were well off there were a couple of high quality spincasting combinations available. They were either the Zebco 33 or a Johnson Century.

If you wanted another rod you normally had an old cane pole or cut yourself a stick and attach a line to it with a hook and sinker. You would normally plan on using your spincasting rod with a bobber and cast it out from shore and then use the cane or stick pole right off the bank. In that way you were covering, what we call today, all the target water.

To get to your fishing spot you rode your bike. Your small tackle box and can of worms were carefully placed in either the side metal baskets or the front basket depending on which type you had. You took care to make sure that your can of worms or night crawlers were placed so it would not tip over and spill your bait.

Your rods could now be either carried by hand as you peddled the bike or you could tie them on the frame of your bike. The one thing I can remember about those fiberglass rods and cane or stick poles was that they could take a lot of abuse without breaking. There were bike wrecks and rods falling off of bikes and other accidents and the rods seemed to always survive these various calamities.

Most of your bikes were old, rusty and beat up. Some of them did not have fenders which was very inconvenient if there was any water or mud on the road. Those bikes that did not have chain guards on them were particularly troublesome. Occasionally this necessitated having to extract pants legs out of the chains.

I overcame the rusty part by just painting over it. Usually in the spring I just got a couple of cans of spray paint and repainted the bike. Although silver was my favorite color I did try a couple of other colors. With a new paint job and with the rust covered up it was almost like having a new bike.

The older bikes had those big balloon tires and we did not have gears on our bikes making peddling a bit tougher. As I remember some of the bikes were a bit iffy on the brakes too but that just required a bit of prior planning when it came to stopping. But our bikes, no matter what shape they were in, got us to our fishing spots and that was all that mattered.

BAITS

Have you ever noticed that no matter how many types of bait you might have in your tackle box that there will be a day once or twice a season that you will not have the right bait or if you do, it will not be in the right color. That is the nature of fishing.

Of course countless makers of fishing baits are banking that fishermen will never have enough baits and will continue to buy more. Can you ever have enough? Probably not.

I have a t-shirt that says, "So many lures, so little time." Fishermen understand this all too well. Over the last fifty years that I have been fishing I went from having a meager collection of baits to now having a basement full of them. When I was a kid I had a couple of spoons and spinners and that was it. We mainly fished with worms anyway. However, as the years went on I have acquired a sizable selection of baits and lures.

Fishermen understand how this happens. Since I am primarily a bass fisherman I have several boxes of bass baits. I occasionally muskie fish so that requires a couple of separate boxes of muskie baits. I also walleye fish so I have another tackle box set aside for that. Plus I troll for walleyes and that means I have to have a tackle box of trolling baits. I need to have another tackle box devoted to fishing for panfish. For my fishing trips to Canada I have another tackle box for that as well. Then there is ice fishing and that necessitates a separate tackle box. Additionally I have numerous boxes of extra baits, baits I normally do not use any more and assorted stuff I have picked up over the years.

Now there are some baits that can be used for several different fish. For example, some bass bait will work well on walleyes. However, as only a fisherman can appreciate, it just seems more convenient to designate separate tackle boxes for different species. Besides that gives us an excuse, as if we really needed one, to buy more baits.

My wife, the Bass Queen, tells people that she and I do not need a 401K plan. Once we retire she plans on selling off the contents of our basement.

After many years of bass fishing I have come to the point that I only need about a dozen baits. Now of course I have each of them in several different sizes and colors. That of course only makes good sense. But to get to this point required many years of experiments.

When I first started to bass fish I would hear that someone was catching lots of fish on bait called The Boogie. So I would go to the sport shop to buy The Boogie. Once I got there I would find an assortment of colors. Which color would work? I do not know so I would buy several different colors. Then it dawned on me that if I had the right color I could then lose it during a day of fishing. So therefore I needed to buy at least two of each color. By the time I walked out the door I had a bag full of The Boogies. Unfortunately as time has gone on, The Boogie is not one of the dozen baits that I now use regularly but then I would never have known that unless I tried them.

Then there is the crucial moment when you find out that a certain bait or color that you can always catch fish with is going to be discontinued. You need to stock pile them for the years ahead when you know they won't be available. As any fisherman knows this is just being prudent.

I met a fisherman once that found out that his favorite color crankbait he used for walleye trolling was going to be discontinued. He spent the winter traveling to sport shops throughout the Midwest and eventually had over 400 of them. He thought that would be enough to last him the rest of his life. A couple of years later the company reversed itself and began to reissue that color again. I told him to look on the good side; he would never have to spend another dollar on baits again.

One of the things I have found is that baits stop working after a while. I noticed that this happens as soon as you buy a bunch of them. A couple of years ago I found a certain bait that I will call The Softie. For one whole season I slaughtered fish with it. Just as the next spring was starting a store in town had them on sale. Not only was it a good bait but unfortunately it also was fairly fragile and had to be replaced often. The sale was a heck of a good deal so I bought a bunch of them. After that it never seemed to work that well again. I now have a shoe box full of them in the basement.

I have a fishing buddy of mine that tells me that fish get used to certain baits after awhile so that is why they won't work after they had worked so well. If that is the case then I have a basement full of baits that will work again in another ten years or so. I will hold on them just in case that they do.

Every spring as fishing fever starts to grab me I am especially susceptible to getting talked into buying more baits. It really doesn't take much. This last spring two fishing buddies suggested a couple of baits and a kid that worked at one of the sports stores recommended a couple of baits. A guy at the sport show promoted a new bait and I read about another one in a newspaper story. So I bought them all and of course in several different colors. Two of them worked very well, three worked well enough to continue to keep trying with them and two of them were complete duds. I think that it turned ok.

THE FIRST DAY OF SPRING

It was the middle of March and I was getting anxious to go fishing. Of course all the lakes were still locked in ice and the regular fishing season was almost two months away.

I was saved from my mind numbing winter boredom by a phone call. My fishing buddy Scott called.

"I heard that the fish are hitting on the Mississippi River," he said. "Let's go." The words "fish are hitting" was all that I needed to hear. "Ok," I said.

A couple of days later, Scott and I were hooking up my boat to the van. It was an overcast day with a bit of wind. But the temperatures were above freezing and after the long, cold winter it seemed almost balmy by comparison.

I was hoping that this fishing trip was going to signal the official end of winter and the beginning of spring. I have always considered it spring, regardless of the calendar, when I can start fishing in the boat.

As we drove along the Mississippi River toward Red Wing, Minnesota, I noticed that the piles of snow were gone. That always adds to the impression that winter is behind us. The grass was still dead and brown and the woods were gray but that would change soon enough. We were going fishing and that was the first big step towards spring.

At the landing Scott and I got the boat ready to launch and we piled on layers of clothes. It seemed like the temperatures had dropped since we had left home. But it did not matter we were going fishing. Spring is here.

The run from the landing to the dam took about ten minutes. I would have called it brisk but it did not matter once I dropped a jig and minnow overboard. I was now fishing.

About ten minutes went by and I felt a weight on my jig and pulled up to set the hook. I could feel a fish pulling back.

"I got one," I yelled. "I got one."

It was good to feel a fish fight against the spinning rod and Scott netted the fish for me. A few minutes later Scott had a fish and I netted it for him. We caught and released about half a dozen fish when it occurred to us that we might keep a few of them. After that Scott caught a fifteen inch sauger and we put it in the livewell.

I noticed shortly thereafter that the wind seemed to pick up. I mentioned it to Scott and he said that he thought that as well. It felt colder too but that could have been because the wind was stronger. Then one of us caught a fish and we forgot about the wind.

A few fish later I looked up to see a light snow flurry. It wasn't much and probably would go away soon. But how could we worry about the snow when the fish were hitting.

We put a couple more sauger in the livewell. It appeared that the snow fall was getting heavier. But it certainly could not last much longer. The wind rattled the branches of the trees on shore.

We had found a small underwater hump and continued to work back and forth across it. We never seemed to go more than a few minutes without one of us having a strike.

I was netting a fish for Scott when I noticed that snow had turned to big sloppy flakes that were swirling around us, driven by the wind. It was looking like a blizzard to me. Then one of us caught another fish.

Snow has a culminating effect to it and once when I was dropping another fish into the livewell I noticed that the ground was no longer brown. It was white. We had a snow storm going but the fish were still hitting.

A few minutes later I was standing next to Scott with the net. I could see his fish as just a brown shape in dirty river water. I did not recognize it at first but when Scott got the fish closer I could see that it was about a two pound catfish.

"My dad would want that," Scott said so the catfish went into the livewell. I noticed that the green carpeting in the bottom of the boat was now white. Snow covered everything in the boat. I had never thought of it before but it seemed strange catching a catfish in the middle of a blizzard. A little while later I caught a catfish so Scott's dad was going to get two of them.

The fish continued to hit and we continued to catch them and it continued to snow. At one point the other side of the river was obscured in the whirling snow.

By late afternoon we were running out of minnows and we were cold from the wind and wet from the snow. We had ten sauger and the two catfish in the livewell. All together we had caught almost sixty fish. It was a good way to start spring.

We both were shivering by the time we got back to the landing. We ran the heater on the van full blast all the way home and we still were cold. After cleaning fish I jumped into the shower. A hot shower and a glass of bourbon seemed to help. I looked outside from the warmth of our dining room. Everything was white; covered in snow.

I had been fishing all day in the boat and caught fish. It can't be winter again. It must be spring.

60,000 BTUs

Because I am usually the camp cook on most of our expeditions I have taken a great deal of interest in stoves over the last few years.

Many years ago I switched from liquid fuel type stoves to propane. The propane cylinders are easier to carry than a can of fuel and a lot safer. They are also easier to use. They burn a steady heat and you do not have to pump them every few minutes.

I began with a couple of single burner camp stoves. They were light enough to put in a back pack. Those were in the days that I still did a little back packing. When I went to Canada I took them along for shore lunches. They seemed to be ideal for that purpose since they did not take up much room in the boat.

Although they were compact they had their limitations. Most importantly they took a long time to heat up a pot of oil to fry fish. After you dropped the first fillets in then it took, it seemed, like an extraordinary amount of time for the oil to heat up again so that you could drop more fillets in. It took a long time to get a batch of fish done which was most inconvenient if you had bunch of people to cook for.

Once on a trip to the Boundary Waters with eight people at our campsite and with two stoves going at full capacity it looked like people were going to drop over from hunger before I could get them fed.

The problem was that I was not getting enough heat to do the job. So I bought a two burner stove. Now I had two single burner stoves and my double burner. I thought my problems were over.

Not yet. A group of us were camping on an island in Rainy Lake. The first night I had hoped to use the campfire to grill a bunch of beef strips that I had been marinating in bar-b-que sauce. But it was raining when I was starting dinner. This was no little sprinkle mind you. It was one of those heavy, pounding, soaking rains.

So I decided to cook them on my stoves in a screened tent we were using as kind of a dining area. Again, I could not get it hot enough to cook the meat expeditiously. It had been a long day to drive up there, motor out to the island, set up camp in the rain and now dinner was taking forever. The campers were getting restless. It wasn't pretty.

A couple of years ago four of us went on an extended fishing trip to Kabetogama Lake. A buddy of mine, HoJo, who was on this trip and had been on the Rainy Lake expedition called me to tell me that he had a new stove with an output of 15,000 BTUs. I went "ooh, very nice."

On our first night I had planned on grilling some venison steaks over the campfire but a week of rain before we left made it tough to get dry firewood so we had to use HoJo's stove. His stove worked ok but it still seemed to take too long to get the steaks done. Clearly I needed to find something else.

I began to hunt the outdoor cooking aisles in sport stores and seriously browse through the cooking equipment sections of outdoor catalogs. Then I found it.

I saw in the Sunday newspaper that a store in town had a camp stove on sale. This stove had two burners with 30,000 BTUs on each burner for a total output of 60,000 BTUs. I knew that I needed that stove.

Admittedly this stove was not the type you could put in your back pack. It was heavy and big and mounted on legs. But since my back packing and canoeing days are fairly well over and most of my camping and outdoor cooking now is at cabins and drive to camp grounds this looked to be ideal.

I brought it home and set it up on the back deck of the house. I fired it up and the rush of flame was indeed a marvelous sound; not to mention the heat that burners gave off. I felt like I was next to a jet engine that just started up.

A day or two later my buddy Doug came over to the house. He had been on several of the Boundary Water expeditions as well as both the Rainy Lake and Kabetogama adventures. Before we left to go fishing I dragged him out on the deck and fired up the stove. He was impressed. When we came back home later in the day I took him back out to the deck and fired it up again. He still was impressed.

However, my wife, The Bass Queen, was beginning to lose enthusiasm for these demonstrations. She drew the line when I started calling people up in the evening on the telephone and told them to "listen to this," holding the phone near the stove as I fired up the burners.

A few months later Doug, HoJo and I were on our annual pheasant hunting trip to South Dakota. Part of our tradition on this trip is on Friday night we host the family, whose farm we hunt on, to a fish fry. We set the stove up on their front lawn. One burner would have a huge pan of potatoes frying and the other a pot of oil for the fish. By this time it was dark outside. I ignited both burners. I turned to Doug and HoJo asking them "is this not wonderful?"

They both murmured approval. Doug suggested that we probably got the attention of one of those overhead satellites and right now someone might be wondering if a missile had been launched from South Dakota.

"60,000 BTUs is a beautiful thing," I said.

ALL IS WELL THAT ENDS WELL

When we left home there were no indications of any storms brewing. My seven year old grandson Max and I are going fishing. His grandmother, The Bass Queen sent us off with a "be careful and catch lots of fish." We stop, as is our tradition, and get a couple of hot dogs for lunch.

When we get to the lake, Max helps me get the boat ready and slips on his life vest. After I launch the boat, Max holds onto the bow rope making sure that the boat does not drift off as I park the van and trailer.

It is for us a typical day of fishing. We work the shoreline with ice jigs and grubs below a light float. We are catching fish and have perhaps a little over two dozen bluegills that we have caught and released. As we drift along the bank the float tips up and begins to move. Max understands that this means a fish is hitting the bait.

I set the hook and hand him the rod. He brings the fish in as it splashes on the surface of the lake and tugs against the rod. He is always very happy when he gets the fish in and many times asks for me to measure the fish. He is getting a lot of eight and nine inch bluegills.

It is our last day of fishing together and I want to get as much fishing in as we can. Max is beginning to lose interest and starts to investigate around the boat. It does not bother me that he is moving around the boat. He has his life jacket on and is used to being in the boat so there is no harm done or danger to him.

I am hoping that he can catch a few more fish and I am not paying a lot of attention to anything except Max and I catching fish when suddenly I feel a cold blast of wind. I look up. Dark, ugly storm clouds are building up on the horizon. The wind has picked up and the temperature seemed to have dropped.

"I think we have to leave," I tell Max. He seems fine with that. I put away his rod, lower my pedestal seat and slide behind the console. I turn on the motor and it chugs away but it does not start. By now the wind is getting worse and the storm is getting closer. I try again. The motor will not start. I try again. Still it does not start.

I look up and the skies above us are getting worse. The landing is across and down the lake from us. The only option I can think of is for us to use the trolling motor but then I remember that yesterday, when we came back from fishing, I had not charged the battery. We were only out for a couple of hours yesterday and I knew that we would be out for a couple of hours today so I thought I could wait another day before charging the battery.

Now I began to worry. The battery had to be running low and I was going to troll back to the landing against the wind. It looked like the only option so I turned the boat into the wind and started across the lake with the trolling motor, praying that the battery had enough charge for us to get there.

I am starting to feel a bit of desperation. If we can not get back to the landing and get caught out here in this storm grandma, the Bass Queen and my daughter Lisa, Max's mother, would not be happy with me. On top of it all I remember that we left Max's rain jacket in the van.

It took forever to get across the lake with the wind buffeting us and then heading for the landing. I was starting to get anxious with every passing minute as I looked into the west to see the gathering storm. This trolling motor is taking an agonizingly long time and the storm is approaching rapidly.

Finally I nose the bow of the boat into the short channel that leads to the landing. Although it looked like it would start to rain any moment I knew we would be at the landing any minute or two now and if the charge in the battery gives out I can paddle to the landing. It has been a long time since I breathed such a sigh of relief as I did when I finally pull the boat up on shore and race off to get the van and trailer.

As we are driving home the skies open and rains come pounding down. I say a prayer of thanks to being off the lake. On the way home I make a quick detour to The Boat Doctor. "This can not ever happen again," I tell them. "Do whatever it takes but get it fixed for good."

The next day Kevin from The Boat Doctor calls. "It was the tether cord on your kill switch," he says. "Somehow it got pulled out."

It made sense now. Max had probably bumped it when he was investigating about the boat. It made me feel better that there was not something wrong with the motor but I felt silly that I had not checked the kill switch. It could have been a lot worse if we had got caught out on the lake and could not get back to the landing.

Everything did turn out ok but I learned some lessons. I will always check the kill switch first if the motor does not start and make sure that the battery is charged for each day of fishing and watch little fishermen in the boat a bit closer. Also, it again made me thankful that everything turned out fine. All is well that ends well.

A LAND OF BOATS

Minnesota boasts of having 10,000 lakes and Wisconsin claims to have even more. With all that water in these two states that means there is a lot of boats.

When you start to count all the pleasure boats such as yachts, pontoons, sail boats and runabouts and add that number to all the fishing boats from the basic aluminum boat with the bench seats to the fancy bass and walleye boats, it makes for a lot of boats. As well we have to count all the canoes, kayaks, duck hunting skiffs and I suppose we should count the jet skies too.

I own two boats myself; a canoe and a fishing boat. I know of many people that own more than that. I swear that it is a requirement to have at least a pontoon boat and canoe for every lakeside home or cottage. That is a minimum requirement. I see some places that have a boat to tow water skiers and a separate boat for fishing in addition to the mandatory pontoon boat and canoe as well as a jet ski or two. We are truly a land of boats.

However, I have found a place that has even more boats. It is Venice, Italy. For those who live there boats are a way of life for them.

Venice is spread out over 118 islands with over 150 canals that weave themselves around and through the islands. There is no motorized vehicle traffic allowed in Venice and as far as I know it is the only city in the world that is completely free of it. In the two days that I was there I never even saw a bicycle. So the only way to get around is either by foot or by boat.

We got to Venice by air, landing at the Marco Polo International Airport which is about four miles outside of Venice. To get from there to Venice requires taking either a taxi or bus just like any other large international city. The difference is that these taxis or busses are boats.

After picking up our luggage we walked about a mile to the water where the docks became the water taxi stands. We were in a group of over thirty so we were divided into two water taxis to take us to our hotel. Although the water taxi drivers are driving boats instead of cars, these taxi drivers are no different than any other taxi driver in the world. They drive very fast with little concern about anything else. I stood in the front of the taxi, outside of the cabin. It was just me and the driver. A water taxi that holds over fifteen people is a fairly substantial water craft and he was racing down canals at a good rate of speed squeezing between the sides of the canals and other boats. I would have been reluctant to take my seventeen foot Alumacraft through that and if I did it would have been a lot slower. To be a truly successful taxi driver you must thoroughly terrify your passengers. It is no different in water taxis.

In the morning you see the delivery boats making their way through the canals. Everything that is needed in the city is brought to it by boats. There is food delivery boats piled high with boxes of produce, cases of canned goods and all manner of fresh meats, eggs and other things that we are used to seeing being delivered by truck. Another group of boats brings the drinks. Cases of wine and water are stacked on the boat as well as kegs of beer. No matter how haphazard it may look I never saw anything fall off.

The official functions of city life are done by boats. I saw police boats and there were even garbage boats picking up the city's waste. I watched as they delivered mail by boat. The boat just pulled up to the shore and the mail man rummaged around the boat like my mail man does in his truck, found the packages and letters he had to deliver and left them on the ground on the side of the canal. I saw an UPS boat. It wasn't brown. It was painted blue but the steering tiller was brown and bore the UPS logo.

I saw a lot of fancy looking wooden boats much like the Chris Crafts and others I have seen from old photos taken in the 1940's and 50's on Lake Minnetonka. Maybe they were all shipped to Venice. Obviously there are no auto mobile repair shops in Venice but I did see a lot of boat repair places.

Of course what would Venice be without its gondolas? At one point before motor boats, everyone in Venice used gondolas. But since the water taxi and water busses came along the gondolas are for the most part reserved for tourists. So we had to go on a gondola ride. It was a windy and rainy day which is not real conducive to gondola rides so we saw a lot of gondoliers just hanging around looking dejected. They got real excited when our whole group decided they wanted a ride.

They put six of us to a gondola and I am here to tell you that they are not much more stable than a canoe. Making slight adjustments in our seating got to be rather exciting. I was wishing that I had brought along a rod and reel. I am sure that would have given our gondolier something to talk about later on with his gondolier buddies. He didn't sing either. I offered to make up for it by singing Drop Kick Me

Jesus Through The Gold Posts Of Life but the other riders in our boat did not seem too enthused with that idea.

As busy as the city of Venice is, it was quiet and relaxing as we glided silently between these ancient buildings. It seemed similar to the hushed reverence of floating along a northern lake at dusk with the pine trees towering along shore. I still wished I had brought along a spinning rod.

PERSISITENCE AND PATIENCE

I thought the wind never stopped blowing in North Dakota but I was wrong. It is a hot and steamy day in mid summer with a few white stringy clouds hanging in a bright blue sky. There is no wind and Devils Lake is stretched out in front of us, the surface flat and undisturbed.

It was late morning by the time Doug and I get out. Yes, I know that in the heat of summer it is said that the best fishing is either early or late in the day. But Doug and I are on vacation and we see no need to beat ourselves up getting out early. Now we don't mind staying out late on the water but this getting up early sounds like work to us and we came to Devils Lake to get away from work and go fishing. So we have a long and leisurely breakfast that will last us all day and then start to get our fishing equipment ready for the day.

As we are loading Doug's truck with our gear, John, the owner of the resort where we are staying, walks by and asks if we are "getting out at the crack of noon?" We might be getting out late but we are going out and we are determined to catch tonight's dinner.

We drive the mile or two to where Doug's boat is pulled up on shore. Just loading the truck at the resort and unloading it at the landing and getting the boat ready makes us break out in a sweat. The last couple of days it has been hot but windy, so it did not seem too bad on the water. The surface of the lake was ruffled by the wind into a classic walleye chop. Today it is flat calm.

Our goal today is a fish fry this evening. As we motor away from the landing Doug and I wonder what the lack of wind will do to the fishing. Doug pulls back on the throttle of his boat and we slowly come to a stop in the quiet water. We are in about thirty feet of water where we had caught fish the last couple of days before. Doug and I believe that we might as well start where we last caught fish and take it from there.

We are trolling bait rigs with leeches. Again it was what worked earlier so it is a good start point. Doug picks up a small fish and then I get a small fish. One good thing about not having any wind is that it is easier to maneuver the boat with the trolling motor without being blown around. But the fishing is slow. We catch and release about a half a dozen small walleyes and drink a couple of bottles of water by the time we catch our first keeper fish.

Doug puts the first fish in the livewell. It is a start towards our fish fry. Then we catch a handful of smaller fish that we put back in the water. We are not going to give up. We want to eat fish tonight. I finally catch a keeper and it goes into the livewell and I remark that we are half way to a fish fry.

The afternoon stretches on. We catch more small fish but nothing for the livewell and I remark that we are still half way to a fish fry. There is a pile of empty water bottles building up in a corner of the boat. It is hot and oppressive and we remark that it sure would be nice to see a little wind.

We talk about moving and we consider changing baits but finally decide to stick with where we are and what we are using. We do know that what we are doing is working although not as well as we might have wished. But we are catching fish so we might as well continue to hang in there. We just got to give it a bit more time.

Finally we catch another keeper walleye. One more fish and we have our fish fry. We just got to keep with it. What we are doing will work. A few smaller fish are caught and released but we are not giving up. We are going to have our fish fry.

It is now late afternoon and we finally catch another keeper fish. We are going to eat fish tonight. We are hot, sweaty, sunburned and out of drinking water. It is time to go find some air conditioning.

We clean fish, take showers, change clothes and sit in the air conditioning, watching the weather forecast on the television. We can expect more of today's weather tomorrow.

I am drinking a bourbon and water and am about ready to start frying the fish when it hits me. In today's world with all of our advancements in fishing technology, new techniques, baits and equipment that perhaps the most effective part of catching fish has nothing to do with all of these modern innovations. Instead it has everything to do with the simple values of patience and persistence. Keep trying and never giving up still counts for catching fish.

NETS

There are those rare moments when you need a net. When you really need one you really need one. But the rest of the time they just seem to get in the way.

Nets are an insurance policy of sorts. It means that once you get a fish to the boat that you have a reasonable chance of getting it into the boat. There is nothing worse than getting a big fish alongside and trying to land it without a net to eventually lose it. This has happened to us all. Therefore we all end up carrying nets in our boats.

I have a large net that I use for northern and muskies. Especially for those two fish, having a net seems to be prudent. Not only do you normally have a big bait with several large treble hooks in the mouth but these fish also have lots of sharp teeth that can do serious damage. I like to keep the bleeding down to a minimum and would much prefer fish blood on my hands then my own blood. Using a net for northern and muskies reduces the opportunity for me to lose any of my blood.

I have a smaller net that I use for walleyes and bass. Since there is also the possibility that I could catch a large northern or muskie while I am fishing for these other fish, my net is large enough to handle them as well.

Normally for bass I am a catch and release guy so if I lose a fish or two alongside the boat I normally don't care. I look at it as just a quick release that does not require me to get my hands dirty. However, a big bass is different. Although I know that I will release the fish anyway, I still want to get the fish in the boat for the photo op before I put it back in the water.

Walleyes are a little different case. I look at walleyes as a food fish and carry a net when I am fishing for them. So if I get the fish alongside the boat and it is big enough or small enough, depending on the regulations or slot limits, then I want to put the fish into the livewell. Losing a keeper walleye while trying to land it is kind of like throwing a t-bone steak overboard.

Except for those times you need the net to land the occasional fish; they just seem to get in the way otherwise. You end up walking all over it if you lay the net on the floor of the boat or tripping over it if you try to put it aside. Once you get another person or two into the boat with several more rods, a couple of tackle boxes and perhaps an ice chest with drinks and lunch there just isn't a lot of extra room. Throw a net in there too and there is all that more stuff to stumble over.

One year, one of my fishing buddies tripped over a net on the floor of the boat and almost fell overboard. This would have been most inconvenient. Not only were the fish biting and his splashing around the side of the boat would probably scare off the fish but also it was early spring and the temperatures were just a hair over freezing. It could have been a very chilly experience.

One year in Canada we came back to the resort in the early afternoon after catching our walleyes for dinner. We cleaned fish and planned on going out after northern pike until dark. Two other buddies wanted to go with me so once we loaded everyone and their equipment in the boat I realized we did not have much extra room. So I took out my big northern and muskie net.

We followed a river to a shallow lake some distance from camp and started casting. We had been fishing for about an hour when there was a huge swirl as I retrieved a large spinnerbait through a weedy patch of cover. When I set the hook the water exploded and I could see a northern pike longer than my leg tearing off.

I quickly turned the fish to get it out of cover and into open water. The fish raced off, pulling line off the reel as my casting rod was bent in half. I would stop the fish from running, turn and start getting it coming back to the boat when it would charge off again. It was a spectacular fight that would last several minutes.

Finally I was getting back more line than I was losing and then it dawned on me that I did not have the net. This is always the wrong time to realize this but this is always when it happens. My decision to take the net out of the boat was a good idea at the time but does not seem so good now.

This northern pike was also the biggest northern I had ever caught up until that point. I planned on releasing it once I got it in the boat but I really did want to get a photo of me holding this fish. As I was starting to get the fish closer to the boat with the possibility of landing it, I was becoming less than enthused with the idea of sticking my hand near all those teeth.

The fish was now alongside the boat. I still was not sure what I was going to do when I remembered that I had a set of neoprene gloves under the front deck. We shuffled around the boat so that one of my buddies could get to the front and get the gloves. Holding the rod with one hand he slipped the glove on the other hand and after switching hands with the rod he pulled the gloves on the remaining hand. I handed him the rod, took the line, and grabbed the fish by the gills, dragging it into the boat. This was a powerful fish and it let it be known by thrashing around considerably while I pulled the hook out and held it up for the photo.

As I was slipping the fish back into the water I wondered would I have ever caught this fish if I had the net. Perhaps, but it sure would not have been as exciting.

WHEN THE LIGHTS WENT OUT

It was sometime in the first quarter of Monday Night Football when the power went out. As far as I was concerned this was most inconvenient. I wasn't necessarily concerned with our losing power. Those things happen. But if we were going to lose power anyway why could it not have waited until after the football game?

We were living in the Appalachian Mountains in North Carolina. It was early winter and periodically, especially in the fall, winter and spring, we would occasionally lose power. It sometimes happened in summer too but I was usually gone for most of the summer so it didn't affect me. Besides football season was not going on during the summer. Losing power was just part of living in the mountains.

I didn't think much about it at the time and was just bummed about having my football game interrupted so I went to bed. The next morning I got up, realized that the power had not been restored so I could not make coffee and was expecting to see my wife, Peggy, who would be coming home soon from her work as a night nurse at a local hospital.

I heard the van coming up the driveway. We lived at the top of a hill but the car never got to the top so I thought that I had better check to see what had happened.

When I stepped outside I realized what the problem was. Everything was coated in ice. I heard Peggy yelling and I started down the hill, slipping and sliding. She had stopped the van half way up our driveway because it would not go any further on the ice. She had gotten out and was now on her hands and knees trying to crawl up the driveway. I got to her and we both ended up crawling up the driveway to get into the house.

As I would soon learn this ice storm had settled across the Appalachian Mountains and knocked power for many counties around us. Power crews were out working but it would be awhile before power would return.

It is amazing the things you take for granted that you do not have once that you lose power. You don't have water, you can't flush toilets, you can't watch Monday Night Football. Schools were closed and that made the kids happy.

But everything was alright. It never got real cold in the mountains and we heated with a fireplace and kerosene stoves so we would have heat. We had enough food in the house. I was concerned about having enough beer on hand but once I checked I found I was good with that.

I had heard of these power outages before and heard the stories that they could last up to a week or longer. I had taken some precautions and had stockpiled supplies to include jugs of water so I thought that this would be alright. Just a mere inconvenience like losing Monday Night Football.

Through out the day the kids all huddled in the family room with the fireplace. That night for dinner I took wire hangers, straightened them out and used them to grill hot dogs over the fire in the fireplace. This got the dog fairly excited and she ended up getting a few of them but at least we had hot food for dinner.

The kids brought down blankets and I had a couple of extra sleeping bags so everyone slept on the family room floor in front of the fireplace to stay warm. As the kids were sleeping I was reading a book by flashlight when it started to fade. This was no problem. I had planned for this and had a pile of extra flashlight batteries. So with the fading light I went into the laundry room where I had stored them. I pulled open the drawer and was seriously dismayed to see it was empty.

I knew exactly what had happened. My oldest daughter Lisa had found them. I raced back out to the family room and woke her to ask what happened to those extra batteries.

"I needed them for my boom box," she said. "We got to have tunes."

It took about three days before our power was restored. It really wasn't so bad. We had heat and cooked our food over the fireplace and life was ok. I did need to get more batteries, however.

On the second night I took all the kids out to the front lawn. It was completely dark. Below us was the small town of Boone and normally there was always a pink haze of light that could be seen from the town. But not now. It was totally dark. We stood on the front lawn surrounded by the woods on top of our mountain. That night there was a cloud cover that hid the moon and stars and everything was black.

I wanted the kids to see this and to realize that this was the way it was two hundred years before man lived here and before the days of power and lights. This darkness was normal for centuries and this was the way it was before we came here.

I am not sure if the kids appreciated it or not or understood it. But we are surrounded so much by light and the civilization that comes with it. It is good to see what it once was like when there was no man made light; just the land and the trees, the quiet stillness, all encompassing darkness and the beauty of night.

GOOD FISHIN' GRAM

Her name was Ethel Beyer. She was 97 years old when she recently passed away. I knew her simply as Gram. She was a quite a lady.

She was my son-in-law's grandmother and I had the privilege of knowing her for the last ten years. When my oldest daughter Lisa married Brian our families came together. That was how I met Gram. From the very beginning my wife, The Bass Queen and I always called her Gram. She was a grandma and a great-grandma so she deserved and had earned that title. Everyone called her Gram so we did too.

She once asked if I knew her first name. I told her "sure I do. It is Gram."

She had lived all her life in east central Wisconsin. Her parents were originally from Hungary but were living in the United States when she was born. Her parents had a farm and the man she married had a farm so she spent much her life on farms. She knew all to well the hard work that was a part of farm life.

I always enjoyed hearing her tell the stories of threshing time when she would have to get the chores around the farm done and still get lunch and dinner out to the fields for the threshing teams. Her descriptions of the food she made would make my mouth water. We are talking hearty food for people who work hard outside all day.

By the time I got to know her, she and her husband had long retired from the farm, her husband had passed away and she was then in her late 80's.

What I will always remember the most about Gram was that she loved to fish. This was not a mere hobby to her. This was her passion. I am sure that initially fishing was part of farm life and putting food on the table but the fun of fishing never left her. She would eventually fish in northern Wisconsin and Lake Michigan and by the stories I heard she was a good fisherperson and always caught more fish than anyone around her.

When my grandson Max came along he became her first great-grandson. She had two older great-granddaughters and my daughter would eventually give her two more great-granddaughters in addition to Max.

Max was about three when I first took him fishing. Gram and her daughter Nancy lived on a pond in Marion, Wisconsin and that was where Max and I went fishing. I got Max a couple of cane poles. Gram and Max's other two grandmas, Nancy and The Bass Queen and his mother, Lisa sat in lawn chairs as Max and I walked out on the dock. I casted the bait out for Max and handed him the rod. In the next half an hour we caught about ten bluegills. Five of them were nice sized fish and were put in a bucket. But Max was only three and after a bit he lost interest which is not unusual for three year olds.

Gram had been watching this with a lot of interest from her lawn chair. After we came in she mentioned how that cane pole looked so light. I asked if she wanted to try it out. I think she was waiting for me to ask her that and she immediately accepted. She grabbed the cane pole and walked out on the dock. She sat down at the end of the dock, baited the hook and flipped the line out. In a moment the tip of the cane pole began to bounce and a bluegill splashed the top of the water. She unhooked the fish, dropped it in the bucket, baited her line and cast out again. In the next hour or so she put another seventeen fish in the bucket and that night Gram, Nancy, Brian and Lisa had a fish fry. Gram was 92 years old then.

A couple of years later she went through a series of small strokes that would finally put her in a nursing home. But she never lost her passion for fishing. She talked often of it and in the last couple of months before she died, when she had trouble recognizing members of her own family, her granddaughter showed her a photograph of some fish that were caught on a recent vacation. She perked right up when she saw the photos and mentioned what nice fish they were. The passion was still there.

She died in early September and we gathered on a warm, early fall morning bright with sunshine and the first colors on the leaves. At the visitation prior to the funeral we paid our last respects to Gram. The tip of that cane pole she caught those fish that afternoon on Marion Pond was inserted into the flowers on top of her casket. On a table nearby was another flower arrangement that included a tackle box. The Bass Queen and I had sent flowers and our card read "Good Fishin' Gram."

The photo boards spread around the room told her life story in photos that spanned her lifetime. There were photos of her with the horses and tractors on the farm and with her family and friends she loved so dearly.

I was amazed at how many photos showed her fishing and holding fish either by herself or with her grandchildren. At the grave, the top of her vault had a leaping bass engraved on it. She might be gone but her passion for the people she loved and her days on the water were not forgotten.

She had worked hard and lived well. She was a great lady and a good fisherperson. There is no doubt in my mind that she is fishing right now in much better waters and still catching more fish than anyone around her.

Good fishin' Gram.

A CHANGE IN PLANS

This trip had been planned for some time. There had been a number of emails back and forth and then some phone calls. William had a few days off work and said that we should go north and fish for smallmouth bass.

He said that we could stay at a cabin that his wife's family had. So on a warm, sunny spring day I followed William to the northeast corner of Wisconsin. We had caught about a dozen smallies the first day; however William said that the water was still just a bit too cold.

That night William, his wife Stacy and I grilled steaks and ate them on the porch watching the sun go down with the colors of the sinking sun reflected in the lake in front. After dark we sat inside and drank a little bourbon. William and I had once worked together a few years earlier and we caught up on the news about some people we both knew. We talked about our families and what had gone on since the last time we had been together and we talked about fishing.

The next morning after we had breakfast, Stacy gave us both a hug and wished us good luck as we left. The plan was to go fish for smallies again.

On our first lake we found that the water was low. We tried to launch William's boat and although we could do that, the problem would have eventually been whether or not we could get the boat back out. It didn't look like we could. So we gave up without launching the boat and moved to another lake.

The second lake was not any better. We looked at it carefully and decided again that although we could launch the boat we might not get it back out at the end of the day. Even with William's four wheel drive it did not look good.

The third lake looked much better and we finally launched the boat. We worked several promising bays in the next hour and we each got one nice smallie but that was all.

Although the last couple of days were warm and sunny it just wasn't enough to warm the water to those temperatures that would trigger activity by the smallies. It had been a long, cold spring and we were still feeling the effects of it.

William apologized for the poor fishing. I told him that there was nothing to apologize for. That is why we call it fishing instead of catching and besides we were having fun regardless if we caught fish. That is all that two fishing buddies could ask for.

But William was determined to find fish. He made some phone calls and finally announced that he knew of a lake that might have a bunch of crappies that were active. It wasn't smallies but we should catch some fish he said. He had a friend that had a boat on the lake already and William's father was going to meet us there. We stopped at a bait shop and picked up a bucket of crappie minnows.

Once we got to the other lake, William pulled out a couple of long ultralight spinning rods. William's father, Shep, met us on the dock as we were crawling into the boat. Not only do William and his dad look similar, they also share the same quick, sharp wit. Regardless if we caught fish or not it had the makings for a fun afternoon.

We had pulled away from the dock, slowly working the shoreline with the trolling motor. William picked up the first crappie and a few minutes later I caught one. They were a little small so we released them. William said that since we were there he wanted to keep enough for a fish fry for his grandparents.

The crappies hit readily and often two and sometimes all three of us had strikes at the same time. The fish splashed to the surface and darted for deeper water. Ultralight rods were bent and the larger fish fought hard. We started to put some crappies into the livewell and it looked like William's grandparents were going to be eating fresh fish that night.

The banter between Shep and William kept us laughing. I felt honored to be dragged into it as well. This little lake was tucked down between some high ground and stands of pine trees. The late spring winds could not get to us and the sun shined brightly and it was warm enough to be fishing in short sleeved shirts.

We caught probably about fifty fish; mostly crappies, a few bluegills and an occasional small bass. We had kept about a dozen of the larger, slab sized crappies. Once we saw the long shape of a muskie cruise by just beneath the surface of the water. William did his best to get the muskie interested in a big plastic lizard but the big fish would have none of it.

It had been a fine day of fishing. It might not have been exactly what we had planned when Stacy was waving at us as we pulled out of the driveway that morning. But we had caught fish. In fact we caught a bunch of fish. We had laughed and joked and told stories and had a lot of fun. What more can you ask for from a fishing trip.

Of course it is always nice when plans work out but when it doesn't, a change in plans can be fun just the same.

BANANAS

Have any of you ever heard that bananas were bad luck for fishing? I had never heard of this before until shortly before I left for a fishing trip to Alaska.

We planned to go out on the ocean for halibut. Just before we left The Bass Queen was doing some internet research for me on halibut fishing. She is my computer wizard and good about looking things up on the internet and takes a great deal of interest in my various fishing adventures.

As she was reviewing several sites on halibut fishing she found one with suggestions of things to wear and take along while halibut fishing that stated explicitly not to bring bananas on board if you were packing your lunch. It emphatically declared that bananas were definitely bad luck and any bananas found would be immediately thrown overboard. It even went so far as to imply that a fisherman stupid enough to bring such an instrument of bad luck on board might also have to be thrown overboard.

This seemed very serious. The Bass Queen asked me if I had ever heard that before. I said that I hadn't. I looked back over the years and thought I remembered people eating bananas with lunch or as a snack in my boat before. I didn't recall that our fishing was bad on those days. In fact, I like bananas and I am sure that I have taken bananas in my boat from time to time.

But this throwing bananas and fishermen bearing bananas overboard got my attention. Perhaps it is a salt water thing, I suggested to The Bass Queen. So when we went fishing several days later out of Seward, Alaska, I made sure that I didn't have any bananas. The water up there was way too cold to get thrown overboard not to mention that it certainly wasn't worth it to go all that way north to bring bad luck to the boat all because of a banana.

I still considered it a salt water thing. Sailors have superstitions that date back for as long as men have been on the seas. However, a recent trip on Lake Michigan made me rethink that as well.

We were trolling for salmon and trout and there was a lull in the action. It was cold and windy so I took a break to sit in the cabin. I remembered about the bananas from my recent Alaskan fishing trip and asked the Captain if he had heard that bananas were bad luck while fishing.

"Oh ya," he said. "It is true."

I asked him how he knew and he told me that when he was a mate on a fishing charter boat that he had an experience with bananas. They were trolling in water where a bunch of other boats were fishing. On the radio they were hearing that all the other boats around them were catching lots of fish but they had not had a strike yet.

Finally the captain asked the fishermen on board if any of them had bananas. One of the guys said that he had and pulled out a bunch of bananas from his ice chest. The captain gave the guy five dollars for them and immediately threw the bananas overboard.

"Within minutes we started catching fish," the Captain told me. So maybe it isn't just a salt water thing.

One night after I came back from that fishing trip I went down to my office and Googled "bananas as bad luck for fishing." I found pages of information and web sites dedicated to discussing the bad luck that bananas can bring to fishing. It is amazing to me the things you can find on the internet.

There were numerous attempts to explain this phenomenon. The two explanations that seemed to make the most sense to me was that bananas spoil rather quickly so that even native fishermen in the South Pacific would not take them while going fishing. They would have to travel some distances to get to their fishing waters and by the time they got there the bananas had gone bad. If this was all you had brought along for food then I can understand their reluctance to take bananas again with them.

Another explanation that seemed plausible to me was that years ago when loading bananas in those old wooden boats it would seem to attract rats and other critters. I can see where that could be considered significantly unlucky.

Recently The Bass Queen and I were in Italy and we met an old friend of mine named David. When I first met him some twenty plus years ago he was the son of an English Army officer and my neighbor in Alabama. David now has a family of his own and lives in France. When he heard that we were in Italy he drove over to see me with his partner, Pam and their young daughter Charlie.

In the course of sitting around one evening Pam told us that as a young lady living in England she had worked on commercial fishing boats in the North Sea. I asked her if she ever heard anything about bananas as bad luck while fishing and without hesitation she said, "Oh yes, they are bad luck."

All this stuff about bananas got me to thinking. Maybe there is something to this after all. Can fishermen in such diverse places as Alaska, Lake Michigan and the North Sea all be wrong? It does make me wonder.

I have decided that it is never worth jeopardizing ones luck while fishing. There are enough reasons that the fish won't bite so why add bananas to the list. I will not have them in my boat anymore either.

SHE COULDN'T SPELL FISH

It has been over fifteen years since The Bass Queen and I got married. When we first started dating she expressed an interest in learning how to fish so I said that I would teach her.

She admitted to the fact that when she was a young girl her father had taken her fishing but that had been many years ago and they had fished from the bank with cane poles. Later she also did a little muskie fishing and been on a couple of Lake Michigan trolling charters for salmon and trout. But for the most part when I first started to take her fishing she couldn't spell fish.

From there she has learned well. She asked lots of questions, carefully observed what was happening and listened intently as I talked while we fished. As time went on she went from not being able to spell fish to becoming The Bass Queen.

She has become a very good fisherperson. She now speaks eloquently about the joys of fishing. She is knowledgeable about the effects of wind, weather and water and where is the best potential spot to find bass.

She has definite opinions on fishing and not afraid to share them. She is primarily a bass fisherperson. She will on occasion fish for panfish but cares nothing for walleye.

One of her favorite baits is the Jointed Shad Rap but she has learned to fish plastics and has become very good with tube jigs. This last season she started fishing sinking plastic worms. She hates spinnerbaits. She has caught some fish on spinnerbaits but for some reason, that I can not understand, she just has something against spinnerbaits.

Of course, because she is The Bass Queen she has her own spinning rods. She has three St. Croix spinning rods for bass fishing. One year she asked for a panfish rod for Christmas so I bought her an ultralight spinning rod and she loved it. How many women would ask for a spinning rod for Christmas?

Although I use any number of different lines on my reels, The Bass Queen will only have one type of line on her reels. She checks to make sure that I am only putting that on her reels. Although she freely admits that she doesn't care to go fishing in the rain, she will fish in the rain if it happens to come up while we are fishing. She has her own rain gear too. One year I loaned her rain gear to another fisherman and he ripped her rain pants. The Bass Queen was not happy with that so I bought her a new set of rain gear. She has forbid me to loan her rain gear out again.

She has her favorite lakes and her favorite spots to fish on those lakes. The Bass Queen also catches a lot of fish now. Of all the people that fish in my boat there are only a couple of them that could regularly out fish The Bass Queen. There are also the days that she catches more fish than me.

It was an unusually hot, early summer day. It had gone suddenly from a cold, wet spring to this bright, sunny day. We were fishing The Bass Queen's favorite lake that I can only identify as Lake X.

The fishing had been slow all day. The Bass Queen was alright with this as she was getting a start on her summer tan. By late afternoon she had six bass and I had two. As is her custom she had been only using a crankbait and tube jigs. I had been experimenting with a number of different baits and they obviously were not working very well.

The Bass Queen sat up in her chair on the casting deck at the back of the boat. She turned and looked across the lake.

"What do you think about moving to the other side?" She asked. "There are shadows on the water against the bank and there should be some fish there."

I agreed that it might be a good idea. I was still experimenting with some new baits and after covering about fifty yards of shore without a strike The Bass Queen suggested that I try a tube jig.

So I switched to a tube jig. On the first cast I felt a fish pick up the bait and began to move off. I reeled up the slack, waited until I could still feel the fish and pulled back to set the hook. I had the fish on for just an instant before the hook pulled loose.

On the second cast I had a tube jig about half the way back to the boat when I felt a fish slam it. It was such a sudden jolt that it almost tore the spinning rod out of my hand. I did not have to set the hook and the fish was running, pulling line off the drag.

I eventually stopped the fish and turned it back toward the boat when it would race off again with my drag whining as it gave out line. This happened several more times but each time I seemed to be getting more line back on the reel and the fish was pulling off less line.

Finally I got the fish alongside the boat and I could see that it was a thick, dark shadow under the water and

I reached into the water, grabbed the fish by the lip and dragged it into the boat. It was about six pounds. It would be our last fish of the day and one of the biggest bass I would take that year.

As we quit for the day The Bass Queen turned to me and said, "Interesting turn of events that I am now telling you where and what to fish with." The Bass Queen has come a long way from the days when she couldn't spell fish.